REAL MEN *do cry*

by Eric Hipple

Former NFL Quarterback
for the Detroit Lions

A Quarterback's
Inspiring Story of
Tackling Depression
and Surviving
Suicide Loss

with Dr. Gloria Horsley and Dr. Heidi Horsley

Quality
of Life
Publishing Co.

© 2008
by Gloria C. Horsley, Ph.D., Heidi Horsley, Psy.D.,
and the Open to Hope Foundation

Third printing 2012

Published by:

P.O. Box 112050
Naples, Florida 34108-1929

Toll Free: 1 (877) 513-0099 (in U.S. and Canada)
Phone: (239) 513-9907
Fax: (239) 513-0088

www.QoLpublishing.com

Quality of Life Publishing Co. is an independent publisher
specializing in heartfelt gentle grief support, as well as
books that educate, inspire, and motivate.

Front cover design by Mark May

ISBN 13: 978-0-9816219-2-0
ISBN 10: 0-9816219-2-9

Library of Congress Control Number: 2008933012

• • •

To my father,
Hoyt Hipple;
and in memory of my son,
Jeffrey Daniel Hipple
(September 5, 1985 - April 9, 2000)

• • •

To my father,
Hoyt Hipple;
and in memory of my son,
Jeffrey Daniel Hipple
(September 5, 1985 - April 9, 2000)

Foreword

men get depression. Men also get bipolar disorder, otherwise known as manic-depressive illness. These brain disorders are serious, disruptive, and destroy lives. They tragically lead to thousands of suicides annually. *Real* men take steps to treat their depression and bipolar disorder should they occur. They battle the stigma. They fight back. This book describes steps taken by one real man — Eric Hipple — as he struggled to navigate his way to learn more about depressive and bipolar illnesses and seek the help needed for himself and his family.

I met and interacted with Eric shortly after the start of this new century. As a sports fan, I knew of his football legacy and had recently learned about the family tragedy that he had faced. For reasons that he describes in this book, he decided to attend an eight-week course entitled "Mini-Medical School on Depression," conducted by the University of Michigan Comprehensive Depression Center. After two months of being flooded with information about the brain, stress, sleep, genetics, psychotherapy, spirituality, medications, and many other topics, Eric learned two important lessons: first, what he needed to do to help himself and his family; second, that by sharing what he had learned, telling his story to high school students, parents, college students, dentists, athletes, and anyone who wanted to listen, he was able to help thousands of others take steps to overcome the still-prevailing stigma.

Part of Eric's story is that clinical depression and bipolar disorder are brain disorders that affect one in five individuals in the world. We now understand them so much better. They commonly start early in life, with symptoms usually beginning during the ages of 15 – 24, and are made worse by the routine stresses that none of us is powerful enough to banish from our lives. The symptoms and signs of clinical depression, described in this book, tend to come in "episodes" over a lifetime, and unless treated, each episode tends to get a bit worse and a bit more difficult to treat. In fact, the World Health Organization has determined that clinical depression and bipolar disorder are producing more burden and disability than virtually all other medical diseases that are known.

Recognizing that new strategies were needed to fight back, the University of Michigan decided to start the world's first comprehensive depression center (www.depressioncenter.org) and take steps to launch a national network of depression centers analogous to the country's network of cancer centers. Major goals of the Michigan Depression Center are to advance research, clinical delivery, and public policy so that we can diagnose these conditions earlier, treat them more effectively, prevent recurrences, and counteract stigma. And that is why the Depression Center arranged to have Eric become a major spokesperson, to spread the word to thousands of others.

Eric shares my viewpoint that to educate and fight stigma, we need more "voices;" many more voices. That is why this book emerged. As a good quarterback, Eric decided to share his knowledge and passion in the belief that he could help explain the game plan to win this struggle and defeat clinical depression and bipolar disorders. Eric knows that with a true team effort, we can — and will — finally conquer them.

— John F. Greden, M.D.;
Rachel Upjohn Professor of Psychiatry and Clinical Neurosciences;
Executive Director, University of Michigan Depression Center;
Research Professor, Molecular and Behavioral Neuroscience Institute

Contents

Contents

Chapter One

From Monday Night Football to Monday Night in Jail

t he year 2000 brought about many changes for me, Eric Hipple. I went from living the high life, known as a former quarterback for the Detroit Lions, to a confined existence as a prisoner of the state of Michigan, Oakland County. Worse, I was a prisoner in my own mind. I still wore a uniform, but I had traded my Lions team uniform for a green, prison-issued jumpsuit. I had exchanged fame and fortune for shame, failure, guilt, and self-loathing. My rights and privileges had been taken away. I worked, ate, read, and lived my life on the schedule of others. I had gone from the locker room to a jail cell and traded teammates for cellmates.

My face used to appear on the evening news in highlights of a glorious game. Now, what people saw on TV was a mug shot of a tired man, a man in pain who truly had hit rock bottom. What those who viewed my mug shot couldn't see was how I had transformed in jail. They wouldn't even suspect that being there was the best thing that could have happened to me, and that for the first time in my life

I was grateful. During my 58 days of incarceration, I had plenty of time to ponder my life. What the hell had happened? Where had I gone wrong?

I hate to admit that I had driven under the influence of alcohol many times in the past few years. Why had I gotten caught this time? I had attended a Monday night home football game. After the game I threw some passes and kicked around the ball with friends in the parking lot of the Silverdome stadium. I signed a few autographs, discussed the plays, and partied with friends at a post-game tailgate gathering. I was on top of the world, feeling no pain, when a sheriff friend of mine suggested he put me up for the night rather than have me drive home. I called my wife Shelly, and she said, "Hey, Eric, you sound okay to me. Why don't you come on home? I need you to take the girls to school in the morning."

I'm sure she was thinking, "Get home before you get into more trouble." Shelly is my second wife and the mother of two of my three girls, Taylor and Tarah. Shelly knew me only too well. "The Hip," as I had been called since high school, could always be counted on for some straight shots — "from the hip" — and unlimited, unrestrained fun. I thought, "What the hell? If Shelly wants me home, I'm there." I started the ignition of my SUV and blasted down the highway toward home.

The next thing I knew, I looked in my rearview mirror and saw flashing lights. Upset, I pulled over, and the highway patrol officer approached the car. I tried to get out.

He said firmly, "Back in the car. Hands on the steering wheel!"

I hesitated, and my mind rapidly processed how I was going to talk my way out of the situation this time. I am Eric Hipple, former quarterback of the Detroit Lions! I call the plays, not this guy. The officer responded, "Now!" His hand on his service revolver convinced me. I closed the door and put my hands firmly on the wheel. The officer peered into the car, took a whiff, and gave me a look. The look was one of recognition, the double-take I often received from fans in the area. I thought, "Should I offer him an autograph or a signed picture for his kids?" I smiled at the absurdity of the situation. He said sternly, "Driver's license, Mr. Hipple." I handed him further evidence of my former glory, thinking I was in the "safety zone," that my fame had worked to my advantage once again. But instead of the expected fan adoration, I heard, "Out of your car, Mr. Hipple." I exited the car in a happy, carefree, drunken state and tried to put my arm around him to steady myself, mumbling, "Hey man, I'm just trying to get home."

Several hours later, an unamused Shelly bailed me out of the county jail and drove me home. By the next morning, news of my arrest made headlines on TV and in newspapers. I realized that those same kids who asked for my autograph after games would now see me as I saw myself: a fallen hero. It was my fame that made me feel invincible, made me feel that despite the thousands of drunk driving deaths a year, I was immune from all the legalities. These same heights of my fame and success made the fall all the more painful.

I appeared in county court the next day. Shelly had gone to work, so I went on my own. I told Judge McKenzie that the whole situation was not really my fault, how Shelly had needed me to come home, and that it was all a mistake. I told him about my other personal issues and the fact that I was a responsible citizen who recognized that I had been impaired. I assured him it would not happen again. I am sure the judge had heard it all a million times before. Denial goes by many names, but it always carries with it the same excuses. Looking back, I truly thought I was calling the plays. The county hearing was difficult, because my mind was consumed by other issues — the business I'd started after retiring from the NFL was in trouble, my wife and I were facing some heavy financial problems, and, worst of all, I was struggling to survive the pain of my son Jeff's suicide the previous year. I did not realize it at the time, but undiagnosed depression and grief were my constant companions.

The realities of having to meet with the probation officer, talk to a judge once a month, and blow in a tube to start my car were more than I could cope with. To the court, I was just another drunk driver, no different from anyone else, just part of the system. To this day, I cannot believe I was willing to use my precious son's death as an excuse for my reprehensible behavior. This was not the life Jeff would have wanted for me, and this wasn't the life I wanted for myself.

When I was in college, I used to go hunting in the beautiful Rocky Mountains of Utah, and I learned the technique of using a "compass tree" to help me find my way in case I ever got lost in the woods. The key is to stand by a tree and look forward in one direction to a large tree still in your line of sight, and walk directly toward the second tree. Once you have reached the second tree, look back to the first tree, then find a third, more distant tree ahead in the forest so the three trees are lined up. Then use the third tree as your next guidepost.

I realized I had lost those skills and become hopelessly lost in the woods, wandering in circles. I had lost my compass tree. I knew I was not making choices that my son would have supported, and I knew my father would never be proud of my recent actions. I needed to realign myself to honor their lives and find my way out of the thicket in which I had enmeshed myself. I pledged to change my life, but first I had to figure out how the hell I had allowed my life to spiral this far out of control and come up with a game plan to get myself out of the mess I was in.

In the football arena, when I was on the line of scrimmage, I often would have a play plan, but then I'd get a feeling and change the play on the spot. I never was one of those quarterbacks who did a 20-play drive. I always wanted to surprise the other guy by catching him on an 80-yard pass and scoring a touchdown. I loved being the quarterback, because it gave me the power to call the plays. Just like on the playing field, I really believed I was still calling the plays in front of the judge, and that I could beat the system with the right offense. I refused to take part in any of the alternatives to being locked up that the judge offered me, and my stubbornness cost me dearly.

The judge met my resistance by putting me in jail for short stints *seven* times before he finally had me serve the full sentence. He would sentence me to three to five days for breaking probation, just trying to prove to me that he, not I, was calling the shots. The judge would order me to attend Alcoholics Anonymous (AA) meetings for 60 days. I would go to a few meetings and then quit with a million excuses, and then it was back to court and jail. I was very defiant, so he made it difficult, and he could hang tough from his bench a lot longer than I could from the defendant's chair.

I was angry, depressed, tired, and grieving. These feelings led to my drinking and overuse of prescription medications, to my decision to drive that night, and to my disobedience of the judge's mandates. In short, these behaviors and feelings led me directly to jail. My teenage son had shot himself, my insurance business had tanked, and my former partners, whom I had set up in the business, had sued me. My personal life was in shambles, but as I saw it, none of this was my fault. Getting up in the morning and brushing my teeth was a major challenge, let alone going to AA meetings and probation appointments. I continued to defy the court.

At that point the judge thought this was a fairly straightforward case of driving while intoxicated — with an inflated ego. Well, in my eyes, he was wrong. With me, the moves were never straightforward. On or off the playing field, no one told "The Hip" what plays to make. It wasn't that I was belligerent, but rather I viewed myself as a free spirit. I was like the poster boy for the state of New Hampshire, proudly championing the state's motto, "Live free or die." The coaches made suggestions during the game, but in the end, as the quarterback, I called the plays as I saw them.

I didn't see why I should attend meetings with a bunch of "losers" who couldn't control their drinking. I couldn't see that off the field I wasn't the quarterback — I was one of those "losers." I had what I considered to be legitimate reasons for my self-medication, reasons anyone could understand: bankruptcy, loss, and, most of all, depression.

All my friends and teammates agreed that the past two years had been a living hell for me and told me I was not only a victim but also a survivor. The company I kept in those days reinforced the false belief that survivors are immune to the rules, to the laws of nature and man. I had been through so much heartache that I was allowed to slip up once or twice. Unfortunately, those patterns of self-destructive behavior became habits that held me down, destroyed my life, and kept me from healing and recovering.

I'll never forget my last day in court when I stood before the bench and the judge looked down at me and said, "Eric, you may be able to beat me on the playing field, but you will not beat me in my own court." He was right. The next thing I knew, I was in county jail serving a 58-day sentence. At the time, I was mad as hell and blamed the judge and the rest of the world for my problems. Now I can actually look back and thank Judge McKenzie.

In some ways, I think I was actually *relieved* when the judge finally sentenced me to the full 58 days. No more probation, no more breathalyzer, and an end to the embarrassing and humiliating process of getting in and out of jail. The deputies would take me out of the courtroom in handcuffs and shackles. When I got to the jail, I would be ordered to change into the green jumpsuit. Just as I would start to adjust to the environment and the food, I would be released. Those short-term incarcerations really messed with my head and stripped me of my agency. God only knows I was already very confused and depressed. Even getting out of bed in the morning and finding matching socks had become a major task. But I still did not see how all of these emotions boiling through me — the anger, exhaustion, tears, guilt, and helplessness — were connected. I was simply relieved that, once in jail, all the plans would now be made for me. There would be no place to go, no bill collectors calling me, no one to bother me. I was protected and apart from the world that now haunted me.

I felt stranded on my own desert island, with the world falling down around me. I could not get off the damn island, and in jail I began to process the realities surrounding me for the first time in two years. Away from all the hype of football, the financial strife, and family issues, I began to focus on the defining events that had led to my downward spiral of destructive behavior and to my jail cell. It was very painful, and as I took a long, hard look at my life, I finally hit rock bottom.

For so long, I had been subconsciously creating problems, major and minor, to distract myself from the central fact that my 15-year-old son Jeff was dead. I would never again see his beautiful smiling face, hear his laugh, or just listen to him talk. All of the happy hours we'd spent together as a family vanished while I was in jail, and I found myself repeatedly imagining the last moments of Jeff's all-too-brief life in vivid detail. I pictured him lying alone on my cold bathroom floor, barefoot, with his big toe stuck in the trigger of my shotgun. Sitting in my cell, I could imagine him pulling the trigger, snuffing out his life, and obliterating half of his beautiful head. Questions and thoughts percolated in my confused mind. Why didn't I catch the warning signs that my boy was in trouble? Why didn't I know how awful he felt? Why didn't I stop this from happening? What kind of a father doesn't recognize that his son is in so much pain?

Even with my constant thoughts of Jeff, the continuity of jail was a respite from my stressful life outside its walls. A blessing and curse of being locked up was that every day was identical to yesterday and tomorrow. My routine required no thought and no decision-making. I helped with cleanup, and I watched television as my inmates argued over the channels and volume. There was small talk on subjects ranging from women, plans for release, being framed, and sports.

Some inmates expressed admiration that I played in the National Football League. Others were less impressed, making comments like, "Man, you're no better than we are." Every night I called my wife, Shelly, from the jail payphone. Hearing her voice always brought me a sense of peace. I missed talking to the girls, as Shelly had asked me to call her after they had gone to bed. Shelly visited me once, and that was enough. I preferred it that way; jail was not a place where I wanted to be seen.

A little more than halfway through my incarceration, several events occurred that would change my life.

• • •

One afternoon I was lying on my bunk, daydreaming and studying the cold cement floor. I counted the cracks running through the peeling, faded paint. As I lay on my bed, my attention was suddenly drawn to a swift, small movement. A cockroach trekked through the debris and slowly made its way around the toilet toward my metal bunk. Suddenly I heard loud banging on the doors of my cell and the cockroach froze. I yelled at my annoying, strung-out neighbor, "Get the hell away from my cell!" The man grunted and moved on. I continued to study the cockroach, still frozen in place. I thought about how much the cockroach and I were alike. I was alone, filled with self-loathing, and frozen in the tracks of my life, trying to make sense of the game. The impenetrable shell of a cockroach protects it from anything, just as my tough emotional exterior had done for me.

● ● ●

I knew then that I didn't need all these tough defenses — the medications, alcohol, distancing — to stay alive. I needed a better offense, not defense, for my life's game. I thought I knew the plays, that I could trust my intuition, find the opening, line up the pass, and release the ball into receptive arms. Warm tears suddenly rolled down my cheeks, and I let myself go. The pain and sadness engulfed me, and my entire body ached as I wept into my pillow. I finally fell asleep in exhaustion. That night I slept better than I had during my entire sentence thus far.

As I approached the dining hall for breakfast the next morning, a guard stepped out from the hallway wall and grabbed my arm, pulling me aside. Startled, I mumbled, "Hey man, I didn't do anything." The guard pushed his intense face up against mine, and his eyes held me in their gaze. A concerned look came over his face as he said, "I know what you are going through. My only son was killed in a gang-related shooting five years ago." He released my arm, and I stumbled as I headed to the table. I was shocked and stunned. Someone actually knew what I was going through, the hell of having my only son die all alone, so young. The guard knew something of the grief, the guilt, the shame, and the endless lists of how it could have been different.

Before, I had felt like I was all alone, the last surviving cockroach after a nuclear blast, but the guard's heartfelt words let me know that there were others out there healing and rebuilding their lives. As I thought of the guard, I realized that he had made it, and so could I. I would no longer lower myself to the status of a bug. I may have been temporarily sidelined on the bench, but my philosophy had always been that when I was knocked down, I had only one choice: to get back up. My life in jail was like a play gone bad — a fumble or an interception and no coach to call a timeout. No referees to reverse the call, and no instant replay. If I was to figure out what brought me here, the replay had to be made in the theater of my own mind. I began to review where it all had started.

Chapter Two

Beginnings of a Dream

I was born in Texas, but I had moved with my parents, two sisters, and older brother by the time I had started kindergarten. We moved to Downey, California, a typical middle-class town, one of the many growing Los Angeles suburbs. I had a happy, somewhat introverted childhood. I spent my summers playing in the backyard pool with my siblings while my mother sat nearby with a glass of wine. I fought occasionally with my siblings, especially my older brother Mike, but there was always a lot of unstated love in our home.

My father was in the environmental cleanup business, as the sales guy who submitted bids for vacuuming trucks, cleaning out oil tankers, and cleaning up oil spills. He had hardly fulfilled the dream he had carried throughout his lifetime of becoming a professional football player. Dad often told me of his desire to become a professional athlete, but once my oldest sister Elizabeth was born, he quit college and the team to provide for his family. However, despite the long working hours and a great deal of travel, he never seemed bitter. Dad was known by all as a fun guy, the life of the party.

From the time I was a very young boy, I received many messages about how to behave in the world and what was expected from me as a man. These messages came from many sources: my friends, teachers, family, and society. I learned early on that it was not okay for boys to cry or show any form of weakness. My earliest memories consist of statements such as, "Big boys don't cry," "Stay strong," "Don't be a wimp," "Take it like a man," and "Don't go getting all sentimental." Similarly, out on the football field it was not uncommon for coaches to yell, "Suck up the pain," "Shake it off," "Get tough," or "Pull it together." While these messages were important lessons for football, they did not serve me well in life off the field. I learned to hide many of my insecurities, pain, and sadness. Instead of reaching out to others for help and support, I stuffed my feelings inside, kept my thoughts to myself, and suffered in silence. After all, I was a man, and I was expected to act like one.

I idolized my dad growing up, and I think he lived a lot of his dreams through me. He loved to hear me talk about the game and never tired of listening to me recount the plays. He sat on the bleachers with my first wife Jann during my days at Utah State and taught her the game. Dad made it to every single game I played throughout my entire football career, except one. I think this was how he showed he cared, as he wasn't one to tell me he loved me. He even went so far as to fly or drive from Los Angeles to the games in Utah. When he had to miss that one college game, he called the field house, and one of the coaches put a radio next to the phone so he could listen to the entire game. I couldn't imagine a better testament of his love and devotion to me.

Like many suburban women in the seventies, my mother was a stay-at-home mom. She was more reserved than Dad, but she provided a stable backbone for the family while he was away. She was like a cautious mother bear, always protecting her cubs. With matters like my interest in football, my father was always the one to say, "Go for it! I'm so proud of you," while my mother was more likely to want me to just be safe and happy. They balanced each other, but Mom was also somewhat pessimistic and cautious, always afraid that I would get hurt. She couldn't bear to attend my games because they made her so anxious about the possibility of injuries. Even through my college and professional career, it was always the same thing: "Are you sure you want to do this?" When I did get hurt, she would say, "I told you so," while Dad would say something to make me feel better, like, "It will be all right," "It's not the end of the world," or "I'm still proud of you." Mom never really got the sports thing.

Sometimes as a kid I'd get discouraged and feel like my sisters, brother, and mom had to sacrifice too much for all the practices, equipment, road trips, and fanfare surrounding football. I used to wonder if it would be better if I weren't such a burden to my folks. I'll never forget the time when I was young, my mother and I were waiting at a doctor's office, and I asked her for money for a vending machine. After I begged and begged, she finally gave me a quarter, but when I put the money in, the machine didn't work. To this day I still feel guilty for wasting my mother's quarter.

I think Mom viewed sports the way she viewed that quarter, putting energy and resources down a hole with no positive returns. If anything, she thought this proverbial soda machine would tip over on me, and I'd end up with a bum knee at 18, unable to get a job and all out of figurative quarters.

My mom was emotionally detached at times, and mornings were hard for her, like me, because she had trouble sleeping. I think I carried with me some of her more negative and pessimistic traits. As a little kid, I would at times go to bed thinking negative thoughts and cry myself to sleep. For some reason, I'd get all hung up on existential questions like, "If God exists, why do so many people suffer?" Or I'd worry about the thought of the word "forever." What did forever mean, anyway? But even if we live forever in Heaven, the thought of forever scared me. What if I were to be sad forever?

Of course, I never mentioned my sadness to anyone, for as I said earlier, I was very good at hiding my feelings. Looking back, I think this was the first sign of my later bouts with depression. I just figured it was all part of growing up. I wonder now whether Jeff and I could have worked out some of his problems if we had talked more openly about feelings.

People always think that athletic kids have it made, but I was a late bloomer. I always felt that I just didn't quite fit in with the other kids, and thus, I was more comfortable around adults. My lack of confidence may have had something to do with the fact that I always tagged along with my older brother Mike and his friends. They would try to ditch me, and one day they tied me to a tree in a walnut orchard so that I wouldn't follow them. On another occasion, they shut me in an old mausoleum when we were playing in a cemetery.

Mike and I would always fight, and he would always win. The tables turned when I was 13 — he put a pillow over my head, and when he turned around, I jumped on his back and wouldn't let go. He never bothered me again. I guess I owe it to Mike that I know how to bounce back. Mike was a good athlete, but he liked to do his own thing so he never participated in organized sports. I respected that about him, but I think my dad was disappointed, which probably made me try even harder. As I saw it, my big brother had the confidence to be opinionated and fearless, and blaze his own trail. It led to many fights, both physical and verbal, between Mike and my dad. Mike didn't take my football seriously until I was drafted into the NFL, and then he enjoyed the attention and the fame from being my big brother.

Again, I don't know whether I was fulfilling my dad's dream or my own, but from an early age, it seemed that I didn't find football — football found me. It wasn't my dream to be a professional. There were many times as a kid I wanted to quit, but the coaches kept me in the game.

From about age 12, I played Pop Warner football. I learned a lot about perseverance from one coach in particular, Mr. Webb. He worked in construction, and unlike a lot of other volunteer coaches, he would show up on time for practice, often in the dusty clothes he'd worked in all day. He showed respect for the game and for us boys. At one point, I had been hit really hard, and it felt like an electric ice pick had been stabbed into my spine. I wanted to quit, but Mr. Webb convinced me that I was valuable to the team and that my presence made a difference. I stuck it out, and I ultimately continued playing Pop Warner and the school's flag football through the end of junior high school.

I entered my sophomore year at Warren High School in 1973. When I joined the football team, we played under a new coach and trainers, and they really inspired me. I pushed myself hard in high school. I spent all summer running, working out, and throwing passes to anyone who would catch them. I made the varsity team my junior year and was the starting quarterback from then on. It was a really heady time — I was captain of the football team, people looked up to me, and they all thought I was self-confident and smart. What they didn't know was the paralyzing fear I felt — not about playing football but about the social aspects of being a teenager.

I often felt like I didn't belong to any one clique. I'd kind of float among all of them, almost like a chameleon. With the jocks, I was posturing and fun-loving, but tough. With the stoners, I'd party like there was no tomorrow. With the nerds, I was a diligent student who knew how to have fun but still earn decent grades. With myself, however, I sometimes wondered who I really was. I'd drift into what I thought of as a "dark cloud" for days or weeks, when I'd feel really pessimistic about everything and totally unmotivated to do much more than go to school and come home. I never spoke to anyone about the pain I was in; I just sucked it up, shook it off, and figured it would eventually pass.

That's when I found alcohol. Booze could relax me and numb that emptiness I felt inside. Luckily for me, we had a fully stocked liquor cabinet, and between my mom and dad's drinking, they never really closely monitored what was in it. I remember using an empty 32-oz. Coke bottle and filling it up every morning with vodka or scotch, so I'd know I had a stash of alcohol available whenever I needed it. We weren't too far from the beach, so during football's off-season, my friends and I would surf and swim after school and during the summers. We always brought along what we called "the refreshments," usually a little something from our parents' liquor cabinets or purchased from the "friendly" liquor store that catered to athletes.

I realize now that I was self-medicating with alcohol, using it to feel better inside. Alcohol was very acceptable with my parents and their friends, and while I wouldn't consider them to have a problem with alcohol, Mom would occasionally pester Dad for drinking too much, and he probably did. Mom was more introverted and quiet with her drinking, and she only drank wine. I don't recall alcohol ever being an issue with them, and they certainly never said anything about it to us kids. Many years later, my dad quit drinking due to diabetes, but my mom still enjoys an occasional glass of wine.

Once the practice season resumed, I'd stay away from the booze to get myself fit. That didn't stop me from joining in the normal high school partying, but my drinking was never too heavy during the season. I felt like I really came alive when I was playing. I loved the buzz in the air surrounding the games. Our stadium was always packed, especially when we played our cross-town rival, Downey High School. The adrenaline rush of a game would keep me feeling high all week until the next game.

After our new coaching team came on board, there was no stopping us. We came out from behind a series of losing seasons and started winning, ultimately going on to the California Interscholastic Federation Championships for our division. There was no better feeling. The transition from a losing team to a winning team fell directly on the shoulders of a man I found to be a great coach and mentor. Frank Mazzotta was a tough coach, yet fair in how he dealt with players. It was his discipline that led us through some of the toughest games and eventually to the playoffs.

One such game came against a team at Edison, which was the largest high school west of the Mississippi. They wore green uniforms and looked like monsters from across the field. Their third team was just as good as our first. At halftime we were taking a licking, and inside the locker room Coach Mazzotta grabbed my jersey and lifted it up to show the rest of the team my ribs mottled with scrapes and bruises from being hit on just about every play. He kicked a trash can over and said, "If Hipple can take it for the team, so can you. We can match these guys!" Even though we went on to lose the game, we gave it our all.

I felt empowered when Coach Mazzotta held me up as a sign of toughness and leadership in the face of powerful odds. I found strength and courage from that experience throughout my college and professional career and even during my later challenges. Coach Mazzotta's enduring high standards for the team and me were a great blessing, but at the time I may not have appreciated it as much.

In the seventies, when long hair was fashionable, he asked the team to vote on buzz haircuts. We submitted our votes on folded pieces of paper as anonymous ballots. After retiring to his room for a few minutes, he announced that the votes had been tabulated, and by majority the team had voted for the buzz cuts. As we took turns cutting each other's hair, we started asking each other how each had voted. About halfway through our haircuts, we found out we'd been had. No one had voted for buzz cuts; the vote was a trick by the coach to set us apart from others. His goal was to make us a team and form a united front. At first I was mad because I thought my hair looked completely ridiculous. But after bonding over the traumatic haircuts, we really became a team, going on to a winning season and the city playoffs two years in a row.

High school is a transitional period in everyone's life, and my experience was no different. I had to deal with the physical changes of my body as well as my mood changes. I continued to be a good student but often felt socially awkward. I was exceptionally lucky to have a strong support system to lead me through those turbulent changes, and Coach Mazzotta was a real rock for me. He showed me just the right balance of care and discipline. Without him, I don't know whether I would have made it through high school, and I know I never would have made it to college. I am still friends with Coach Mazzotta, and he continues to set a tremendous example for me. I often wonder whether my son Jeff would still be here if he had a coach like Frank Mazzotta, and I wonder why I couldn't have been that figure for him.

Chapter Three

College Glory Days

being the quarterback at Warren High School was great. It wasn't until near the end of my last season that I considered the possibility of playing football in college. My older siblings hadn't gone on to college, but because I'd always done well in school, I thought I'd try a semester at our local community college or at Cal State Fullerton, where many of my friends were going.

My plans changed after I learned that a football scout had attended one of the games at which we'd performed really well. The scout actually had been there to watch someone on the opposing team, but I guess I caught his eye, because the next thing I knew, Utah State University approached me to play ball on a full-ride scholarship. Their recruiters showed me spectacular photos of the mountain setting in Logan, Utah, and pictures of the canyons; the availability of outdoor adventures looked pretty enticing to a kid from a blue-collar south Los Angeles community. I also learned from another scout that the University of Santa Clara, in Northern California, was also interested in me. Still, that fresh mountain setting of

Utah State was hard to resist, so I accepted their offer.

At my high school graduation in 1975, I felt like I owned the world. I'd been captain of the football team, started in every game, and had even gone to the championships. Right before school ended, I broke up with my high school girlfriend, and I was feeling footloose and ready for action. That summer, a group of friends and I spent a lot of time four-wheeling out at Kern River outside of Downey, zooming around the sandy desert river beds in a souped-up, open-top VW dune buggy.

One event, however, almost ended my football career before it even began. My friend Jerry and I were heading home from a night out in the desert. Jerry was driving, and I was sitting beside him. We were racing down the road that runs alongside the vast Kern River when Jerry lost control, hitting rocks on the embankment. The car barrel-rolled three times and ended up on its four wheels in the rushing waters of the river. Jerry hadn't worn his seatbelt and was thrown out of the car on the first flip. He landed on the road and sustained some pretty ugly road burns. I was belted in, so I went crashing into the river with the car. I remember hearing a loud "pop" as we made the first flip, and I have a vague recollection of unfastening the seat belt and trying to swim to shore. The next thing I remember is being in the hospital, where I learned that the accident had cracked my skull open, ruptured my eardrum, and dislocated my shoulder.

That was one of those times I wished I could have pushed the "fast-forward" button and skipped a section. My recovery was terrible physically and mentally. I remember lying in the hospital bed, thinking, "Hey, I'm supposed to be reporting to Utah State for summer training in three weeks! This can't be happening!" I wondered whether I'd be able to play football again. My dad, always such a motivator, said, "Sure you will, son. You heal fast," even though the attending physicians at the trauma center said it would be a minimum of a year before I'd be cleared to play. My dad, unwilling to let my dreams die as his had, found a specialist who, after a thorough examination, said, "Eric is ready to go." I was released from the disabled list, so I was ready for action. To my mother's horror, but to everyone else's delight, three weeks later I was on the road to Utah, still healing but ready to play with the pain.

I give my mother credit for still driving with Dad and me to Utah, despite all her reservations about my decision to play. We went a week before the official start time so I could get acclimated to the higher mountain altitude and have a chance to explore and feel at home in this new environment before the intense training began.

I had never lived away from home, and I had a lump in my throat when my family left to return to California. After the initial feeling of being lonesome and abandoned lifted, I remember that sense of total freedom. I could be or do anything I wanted there; it was as if I had no past history. Nobody really knew me. The flip side was a sense of feeling really disconnected and wondering whether I really belonged there. Was I going to be able to make friends? Would I be ready for the university-level academic challenges? During that initial period, however, before the dorms officially opened, I was staying with one of the older team members. He showed me the ropes, and I realized that I was simply experiencing what every college freshman feels.

Then there was football. I'd sometimes feel dizzy during the early practices, especially after getting sacked. This scared me a little, but of course, I didn't let my parents in on my concerns. As time went on, my head cleared, and I felt that I was ready to get back in the game. To my dismay, at the first official practice, I learned that I wasn't the only quarterback they'd recruited; three other guys were ready to show their stuff and take the lead. These guys were really good, and I knew I'd have to be at the top of my game. Every day I'd push myself to improve my personal records. I'd go running up in the canyon behind the campus, taking on the hills and inclines in order to become tougher and faster.

In college football, athletes are eligible to play for only four years, so teams do what is called "redshirting." Ineligible or inexperienced players practice wearing red shirts but don't play in any games, thus, not losing a year of eligibility. I started redshirting my freshman year, yet, incredibly, Utah State played me in almost every game.

I was able to play because Utah State was an independent school; it didn't belong to any conference so we didn't have to adhere to conference rules. We had in-state rivalries with Brigham Young University, the University of Utah, and Weber State, and we were scheduled to play several big schools to increase the team's revenue.

The University joined the Pacific Coast Athletic Association (PCAA) my junior year, and that's when I was officially redshirted for my freshman year. This allowed me to play for five years — I had played officially for only my sophomore year, and I had three more years to play. Is it any wonder that I saw rules as flexible, always with exceptions? For me, the policy was great because I never really had to sit out a year. I played in games my freshman year and was a four-year starter after that.

As in high school, I was extremely blessed with great coaches at Utah State. My second year brought the coaching change that propelled me to the NFL. Our head coach, Bruce Snyder, who came from the University of Southern California, would sit with me and play Xs and Os with magnets and a board. He would show me how defenses worked and how to read coverages, but the biggest and best thing I learned from him was the one rule he set for the team to follow: the "do right" rule. It was his belief that everyone had the capacity and insight to know right from wrong and when you're cheating yourself or your team. How brilliant and simple it was to make me accountable for my own actions by holding the standards up to my own conscience. During my time in jail, I wished I had continued to live by his rule.

Terry Shea was our quarterback coach offense coordinator. He would go on to be head coach at Rutgers and coach in the NFL with the Kansas City Chiefs, Chicago Bears, Miami Dolphins, and with the St. Louis Rams. His humor and passion drove me to become a better player and human being. After my senior year, he gave me a scrapbook of my entire university career. I was so surprised and warmed by his generous gift. Years later, Coach Shea sent me a profoundly comforting and caring note that helped ease the pain after Jeff died. I believe these coaches' dedication and guidance led me to become Utah State's "Quarterback of the Century."

Some of the most memorable games took place on the road against powerhouse teams, usually at their homecoming games. I'll never forget standing on the field at the University of Nebraska, looking at a sea of screaming fans wearing their team's signature color. By halftime we were tied 14-14 and ready to score in the third quarter, but I stretched a nerve in my shoulder that left me unable to move it. We battled hard that day, and later the family of Nebraska's Coach Tom Osbourne wrote me a letter to inquire about my shoulder and congratulate me on a great performance.

Another memorable game occurred on a rainy day at Penn State. It was pouring rain; the water was dripping off my helmet and running down my nose. We played the Nittany Lions and Coach Joe Paterno to a near win, only losing in the fourth quarter after we had exhausted our resources.

Before one away game in 1979, popular Arizona State coach Frank Kush had just been fired, and fans in the crowded audience were stomping their feet and chanting his name in support. Simultaneously, the players on the field showed their support with one of the toughest blitzing defenses I had encountered.

I also remember a disastrous game we played against the University of Miami. With our opening kick, they ran it back for a touchdown. We were out-sized, for they had depth as well as speed. Though we fought back, we weren't used to the Florida heat and lost the game. Several players, including me, suffered from heat exhaustion, but we recovered quickly enough to enjoy our overnight stay in Miami. The next morning, we received a halfhearted lecture from the coaches for being out on the town after curfew.

I always loved playing under the lights. I remember lying on my back gasping for air during one particular game in the night lights with Memphis State. After a forty-yard run for a touchdown, I heard the whistle blow and the referee call out, "Holding!" My eyes teared up with exhaustion and I thought, "How can we do this again? I have nothing left!" But the game went on. Slowly picking myself up, I trotted back to the huddle to line up again. Giving up was not an option. Win or lose, it was the effort and sacrifice that counted.

I was quarterback for one of the best games in college football history, a September 8, 1979 game that held a record for 20-plus years as the highest scoring tie in college football, at 48-48. We were playing a PCAA opponent, San Jose State. Their quarterback Ed Luther was a friend of mine and an opponent since high school. We would finally get our showdown. It was an unusually fast-paced game. San Jose State ran four wide receiver passing offenses, and we ran a roll-out style run-and-pass offense. We had them beat until I threw an interception for a touchdown, and in the last two minutes we had to fight back to tie the game with a goal. Forty-eight to 48, and that's how it stood. I laughingly look back at that game with Ed and figured that I had won the quarterback battle... since I threw one of his touchdowns for him! He later went on to play for the San Diego Chargers.

I'll never forget my first experience with a televised game. We never got TV time at Utah State, but then in 1979 Brigham Young University, breaking all the records, came to town. ABC regional TV covered the game. This was the only game in my career that we beat BYU, and it was televised. What a thrill it was for the entire team. I remember how weird it felt to be interviewed, but I was surprised by how much I enjoyed it. Because I was a quarterback, people saw me as an extrovert, but the real me was shy and didn't know what to say.

I prefer to remember only the glories of football, but unfortunately I also remember the crushing off-seasons all too well. When I was playing, I was focused, and because I thrived in a structured, scheduled, time-challenging environment, I actually performed quite well in my classes. During the fall football season, it was easy for me to stay on top of my class assignments. However, during the off-season (spring quarters), I felt that with the pressure off, I could relax. One quarter, I let my GPA plummet and I had to attend summer school classes to make up for the failed courses. I was clearly in a funk. I couldn't get out of bed, and I never felt well. I couldn't attribute it to anything specific; I just didn't feel motivated. It was hard to sleep, and at times I'd feel exhausted and want to sleep all day. In fact, I basically slept through that whole quarter, getting up at three p.m. and back in bed by nine p.m.

My appetite wasn't normal, either. Especially when I'm training (but, unfortunately, the rest of the time, too), I eat like a horse. I am a big steak-and-potatoes guy. Plus salad. Plus veggies. Plus about a gallon of milk. Plus pie. And don't forget the ice cream! But, for some reason, I just didn't have much of an appetite during these periods. Looking back, I realize I displayed all the classic symptoms of depression, but at the time I had no clue about depression or what I needed to do to get out of the slump. Fortunately, once I'd start training again in the summer, I'd always spike right out of it. I didn't really give these blue periods much thought until many years later, when I reflected upon what my son Jeff had been going through prior to killing himself.

During my third year at Utah State, I noticed a gorgeous cheerleader with the most beautiful smile I'd ever seen. Jann and I soon became inseparable and enjoyed hiking in the mountains, hanging out with her Mormon family, and going out for drives. I loved her family, and they became surrogate parents. I even went so far as having her dad baptize me into the Mormon Church. I never got into their abstinence from coffee, tea, and alcohol, and was only active for a short time, but Jann and our daughter Erica remain active members.

Jann's family lived near the campus in a big, sprawling house, and more often than not, I could be found there playing games, watching TV, and having fun with her brothers and sister. I also enjoyed hunting and target shooting with the guys. Jann and I were young, in love, and impulsive. Despite a lack of enthusiasm from both sets of parents, we decided to wed during our junior year in 1978. Our marriage was especially difficult for my dad, as he was concerned that history might be repeating itself. He didn't want me to be forced to quit football in order to get by.

Even though Jann and I thought things would be easy, we soon learned that two cannot live as cheaply as one. It was hard getting by on my football housing and food allowance, combined with the money

I saved from working odd jobs during the summers. Jann soon dropped out of school and got a job in a flour mill to help make ends meet. We lived in a tiny house trailer in the student housing area of Utah State, along with hundreds of other equally young newlyweds. Regardless of our shaky finances, we had a great time in the early years of marriage, when most of our attention was focused on my football career.

Even after marrying, I seemed to continue to cycle through seasonal bouts of darkness and apathy. I remember Jann getting so angry at me for just lying around on the sofa all day, when she had sacrificed her degree to enable me to continue with school and football. Sometimes I'd tire of being cooped up in our cramped quarters, and I'd head over to my in-laws' big comfy house, where I could stretch out in their family room, hang out with her brothers, hike up in the canyon, or go hunting with her dad and brothers. Eventually, I'd pull my act together and get back to classes, and I was able to end the semester with grades I wasn't ashamed of.

I'd habitually procrastinate studying, writing papers, and registering for classes until the very last minute. Then, somehow I'd be able to perform and make it all work. Maybe I liked the adrenaline rush from the pressure and stress of working against impossible deadlines because it was similar to the rush I felt in high-stakes games. Like many college students, I initially didn't have a clue what to major in. I explored several courses of study, including art and English, but eventually found that I did well enough in business and computer programming classes to earn my undergraduate degree with a double major.

Strange as it may seem, it hadn't really occurred to me that football might become my professional career. I always had thought of it as a way to pay for college while having a blast. But during my senior year, my coaches started talking with some of us about next steps, and they thought I'd be a likely candidate for an NFL draft. As my final semester wound down and announcements of the NFL draft picks were at the top of the sports page each day, I'd anxiously await the news — was I going to be selected?

Even though Utah State had named me Quarterback of the Century and my conference rated me highly, an injury I'd sustained during the last game of the season set me back further in the draft standings. Rather than being a first-round choice, I was in the fourth round, which made waiting for the news even harder. Eventually, it came down to two teams: the Detroit Lions or the St. Louis Rams. I was almost certain it would be the Rams. Jann felt really comfortable in St. Louis because she'd lived there while her dad had attended dental school. At the final hour of the final day of the draft, I learned our next destination.

Chapter Four

Winning Seasons
with the Detroit Lions

J oining the NFL and the Detroit Lions was an absolute thrill for
me. Jann, however, was skeptical about living in such an urban
area. From day one, I felt like I was born to play on that team. I had
benefited from excellent coaching in high school and at Utah State,
and I approached my professional career with the same dedication
and enthusiasm I had brought to my earlier football seasons. I'd learned
that although self-confidence is important, especially for the quarterback, it was always better to show a bit of humility and respect than
to go in acting like I walked on water.

My coaches had taught me well. Show up on time. Do the work.
Get up when you are down. Stay focused. Put the team first. I think
that all these qualities led the Lions coaches to keep me on the team
and ultimately select me as starting quarterback. Soon after I arrived
in Detroit, I learned that, as in college, I would be competing against
three other talented quarterbacks for starting position. I noticed that
some players seemed to have the attitude, "I'm it." These guys played

to protect themselves from injury and to make themselves look good, and the team's victory came second in their minds. These egos soon got traded. The coaches wanted team players who were tough, smart, and accountable.

Back then, players weren't compensated with the superstar, megabuck salaries they now receive. I was happy making about $50,000 a year my starting season, whereas nowadays top players normally receive multimillion-dollar signing salaries. The salaries and perks were much more modest then, and unlike today's free agents, players tended to stay with the same team throughout their entire career. Most of the team members' salaries were within the same range, so the constant friction that teams now experience didn't exist. Our loyalty to the same team gave us a close connection with our fans. Lions fans were mostly blue collar, and they related to us because they knew we were pretty much just like them.

As the starting quarterback for the Lions, I enjoyed a fair amount of fame. Most of the time this was great, but the occasional rabid fan would follow or call some of the players. I started leaving my hunting rifle under my bed, a habit I would later come to regret. Even though the team had been going through a few rough, losing years when I joined, its strong, loyal fan base made playing really great. We could feel the buzz of excitement in the air during the games; the support from the fans was palpable. I just loved the game, and I probably would have played for free. I felt honored to be part of the NFL and a member of the Detroit Lions. They always were very good to me.

With the arrival of a new team of coaches, we were soon putting together some winning seasons. My Monday Night Football® debut took place in October 1981 in a game against the Chicago Bears, who'd just won the previous Super Bowl®. They were relentless, and our offensive line had been terrible that year. Gary Danielson had been the starting quarterback, but he was injured shortly before this important game, so they put me in. This was my big break. Nobody knew anything about me; I guess we took them by surprise. I threw four touchdowns, ran for two more, and we basically set the whole town on its rear. I was recognized as the best starting debut as a quarterback on Monday Night Football, and my jersey is actually in the Football Hall of Fame for it. Fans in Detroit still remember it and approach me on the street to talk about *that* game. From that point on, there was no stopping us. We were divisional champs once and went to the playoffs twice.

During my third year with the Lions, in the next-to-last game of the regular season, we were playing the Green Bay Packers. With only a few minutes left in the game, I dropped back on a three-step drop and fired the ball to our split receiver, Marc Nichols. It was a perfect pass and a perfect touchdown, but my left leg buckled as a result of a late hit from their blitzing strong safety. Today, rules have changed and you can't hit a quarterback after the pass.

In 1985 the playoff-bound Chicago Bears came to town. With a mediocre season and no chance of going to the playoffs, we knew this was our last game of the year. In other words, it was a lame duck game with nothing to win, except pride. Joe Ferguson started as quarterback while I stood on the sidelines with a bandaged left leg. As the football gods would have it, Chicago's defensive end sacked Joe just three plays in and knocked him out of the game. I thought, "Are you kidding me?" I could hardly drop back, much less play against the best defense in the league that year. But there I was on the field; I was still that kid asking my body to "suck it up" and telling myself, "Be a man!"

During the first series I participated in, I decided to go for the deep ball and score quickly. The ball snapped, and I backpedalled (due to the pain in my knee, I couldn't turn sideways to drop), looked deep, and let it fly. As the ball flew, I felt the rush of adrenaline, with the possible touchdown looming downfield. But a Bears defender Dan Hampton intercepted the pass. I thought, "Tackle him," and the crowd started to boo with every step as the Bears defender approached our end zone.

Then it dawned on me that I, the injured one, was going to have to make the tackle. I started with a little hobble but soon loped into some sort of awkward gallop. That's when it happened: Two monster hands grabbed my shoulder pads, jerking me to a sudden stop. The boos were getting louder in the background, but my attention was focused on the six foot, seven inch, 300-pound defensive end who had just frozen me in time. With both of us standing there looking at each other, he gently said, "Eric, if you stop right here, I won't hurt you." The boos continued to grow, as it looked like the interception was going to turn into a touchdown. "Okay," I replied, "but can we make it look good?" "Well, sure, why not?" he said, and with that we both slowly shuffled toward the returning interceptor, his hands never loosening their grip. "Thanks, Dan," I thought. The guy did get tackled, but the Bears went on to win not only that game but also the Super Bowl. Thank goodness there are true champions in the league. Dan made it possible to avoid what could have been a serious re-injury of my knee, and instead I was able to go on and play six more seasons.

The 10 years I played professional football were the best years of my life. I loved the game, and I loved the team. But playing football wasn't the totality of my life. After I had been recruited by the Lions, Jann had stayed behind in Utah while I attended training camp. Shortly after the season began, she joined me in Michigan, and we settled into a great community outside of Detroit, not too far from the Silverdome. Jann soon made friends with the wives and girlfriends of my teammates, and we'd often socialize together with barbecues, vacations, and, of course, road trips for the games. Jann did a bit of modeling and kept busy setting up and decorating the beautiful home we'd purchased. Two years after I began my professional career, Jann and I started our family with the arrival of our daughter Erica.

Sometimes I'm asked if she was named after me, and I have to laugh. Even though I wish it were true, my wife was actually a big fan of the soap opera *All My Children*. Erica was the main character, so Jann had always promised herself she'd give that name to her daughter. Two years later, we welcomed a son, Jeff, to our family. We had a lot of fun during those early years in Detroit, and our kids were the unofficial niece and nephew of my teammates and their wives. There was a lot of camaraderie among the players, and we also were active members of our local Mormon church.

The flip side of all the family fun was the life of the professional football player, and it was pretty wild during that period. Parties followed each game, especially after the away games when NFL wives were home with the kids. I remember one time during the draft when someone arranged for a "paid escort" to arrive at the hotel door of every team member. These were the days when the booze flowed like water, drugs could be found at every victory celebration party, and partying drowned our sorrows after losing a game. We didn't give it a second thought when we saw a team member with a gorgeous blonde or brunette "date" while we were on the road, and we didn't mention it to our wives.

In addition to all the recreational drugs that were readily available, most of the players had sustained injuries, some of them severe, and were often given prescription painkillers of some sort. This was a recipe for addiction, but the personality of the player determined the nature of the addiction, whether it was alcohol, cocaine, marijuana, amphetamines, or prescription painkillers and tranquilizers. Remember, this was before the "Just-Say-No," zero tolerance, and drug-testing era, so it all just came with the territory of the pro-sports lifestyle. Living in the fast lane was fun and filled with adrenaline rushes as I played with teammates on and off the field. I soon noticed that I was drinking more and more, often combining drinks with a painkiller so I could drink even more, which obviously didn't fit in with Jann's and the kids' lifestyles. The party scene was especially difficult on my marriage because Jann, being a practicing Mormon, abstained from both drugs and alcohol.

During the off-season, we had to stay busy, and most professional players took on some sort of job just to keep their fingers in the pie. With the anticipation that I would not be able to play anymore at some point in the future, I knew I needed to have some alternatives waiting on the sidelines. During these off-season periods, I tended to fall into the blue funks I'd experienced in high school and college.

I just wasn't happy, and somehow I couldn't find the magic combination of adrenaline-charged and leisure activities. Even alcohol or medications wouldn't make me feel like my energized self again. I missed the thrill of leading the team and playing the game. I couldn't imagine having to wake up to a nine-to-five job every day, so the various office and sales jobs I held during the off-season killed my enthusiasm and belief that I could accomplish anything. Perhaps it was the stark contrast between quarterbacking a winning team and toiling as just one more cog in some business or organization where my individual contribution didn't seem to matter much. I would self-medicate and keep on plugging through until training started back up, and then I'd bounce back to my old self again.

Whenever I was asked what advice I would give to those starting out in professional sports, I'd just repeat what Bob Snelker, one of my early Lions offensive coordinators, told us: "Be humble. Don't be a troublemaker. Don't go in with a lot of bravado. You have to prove yourself first." Bob said that players need to be aware that coaches are watching everything, including every pass you throw, whether you sit on your helmet, and whether you pay attention at practice. Even if you're in practice, throw like the game depends on it. Run like you would if you were scoring a touchdown, because the coaches base their decisions on who to play or who to cut on all their observations, not just on how you did in the last game.

Through the years, I'd hear people say that what my coaches and fans liked about my style was that I seemed formidable. I didn't dodge a hit if it would hurt the game, and if I was knocked down, I got right back up. Everything was for the team. I didn't really care about my own stats as much as I did whether we won or lost. I think that's the mark of a good teammate and also the mark of a leader.

Even though I'd bounce back from the blues with the start of each training camp, every playing season was not a bed of roses through those 10 years with the Lions. Like all quarterbacks, I was a target on the field, and with that time's less stringent rules against hurting the quarterback, I sustained a number of injuries. Even with injuries, I'd travel with the team, sitting in the coach's box to help call defensive plays and identify the opposing team's strategies. Injuries are really the worst thing that can happen to an NFL player, because if they are severe, the team management doesn't want you around the other players. It is bad for team morale to see all these guys hobbling around on crutches or all bandaged up, so if I sustained a severe injury, that was it for the season. I was pretty much forgotten.

At one point, my nose was broken early in the season. My trainers told me to ignore it and wait until the end of the season, because it probably would keep getting broken until it had a chance to fully heal. Another time, back in college, I injured my foot in a game. The coaches gave me a shot of cortisone, taped it up, and I played through the remainder of the season. Only later did I learn that a bone had snapped and was just grinding away all the tendons and ligaments in my foot. I remember being anxious that maybe they'd cut me from the team if I didn't bounce back quickly or well enough, so I would really push myself through the rehab and in rebuilding my speed, strength, and endurance.

I'd learned early on that you just have to play through the pain. You get hit. You get hurt. You just get up and keep going back in. Sometimes you're bandaged, sometimes you're shot up with pain-killers, and sometimes you just play through the pain. I didn't want an injury to force me to quit the game I loved so much; I wanted to be the one to make that call when I felt the time was right. Little did I know that it would come sooner than I expected, and that I would not be the one to make the call. Some injuries can't be taped up and forgotten, and not all healing can be indefinitely postponed.

Chapter Five

Tackled by Life

In 1987, eight years after joining the Lions and moving to Detroit, I found myself increasingly unhappy. Maybe it was that boredom that can set in when we reach a certain rhythm, and it seems like everything is set on automatic. Maybe it was because at that point, I realized that although we were always close to getting there, the Super Bowl was beyond the Lions' reach. Maybe it was all my injuries that were making it harder each time to bounce back physically. Maybe it was that Jann and I had grown apart. I knew Jann was sick and tired of putting up with all the shenanigans that were so much a part of my life as an NFL player, but I wasn't willing to give them up. We tried to hold our relationship together for Erica and Jeff and went to a marriage counselor, but it didn't do us a lot of good. We soon realized that we'd be better off separating. It certainly wasn't what either of us had planned going into the marriage, but people change a lot as they move through the ups and downs of life.

As I reflect on our marriage, I realize how young we really were. Jann was just 19, and I was 20 when we'd married. We literally grew up together — the high points were the births of Erica and Jeff. We'd traveled together, bought a second home on the California coast, taken flying lessons, and enjoyed spending time with our extended families. But as we grew up, we also realized we were on different paths. I was a carefree adventurer, always seeking the next adrenaline rush, ready for action and totally spontaneous. I now realize that this was my defense against depression. Jann, on the other hand, was more pragmatic, practical, and conservative. The last-minute, chaotic nature of my lifestyle unnerved her. After separating and attending sessions with the marriage counselor, we got back together for another go at it. We didn't want to just throw away what we had, but unfortunately our life paths at that point were on such divergent courses that we just couldn't recombine them without one of us feeling totally squashed by the other's unmet expectations.

Jann and I were both fortunate to have parents who had made lifelong commitments and enjoyed very successful long-term marriages, and they were disappointed that we wouldn't be able to provide that for our own children. Divorce isn't something that couples approach lightly, especially when children are involved. It was painful for all of us, especially for Erica and Jeff. Soon after the divorce was final, Jann moved back to Utah, and the kids spent the school year with her and their vacations with me in Detroit. While in Utah, Jann met a guy whom she felt was stable and a responsible businessman, and she soon remarried.

In the meantime, I'd met Shelly, a beautiful woman who worked in the office of an athletic training center. She knew nothing about football, but we soon discovered that we shared a zest for spontaneity and adventures. We dated, and she became my lifeline after my final injury and sacking by the Lions. I was happy with Shelly, and I felt like myself again for the first time in a long while. I'd bought a small

airplane a few years earlier, and we loved zipping off to explore different areas and attending far-flung games. We loved the outdoors and
spent a lot of time on speedboats, scuba diving, and hanging out
with friends who lived in the New York and Chicago areas.

All this time, I'd be playing my hardest, always trying to best
myself, to outdo my previous year's accomplishments. The threat of
being traded was always hanging over our heads, and no matter how
well we had done the previous season, there was an unspoken question: "Yes, but what have you done for me lately?" Unlike other pro-
fessions, in which managers value the experience seasoned workers
can pass on to those coming up through the ranks, as NFL players
we never could rest on our laurels. No, we were expected to perform,
and we were competing against ever-younger and bigger players on
the opposing teams, as well as the young players who were recruited
to Detroit every year, hungry to make their own mark.

During the end of my ninth year with the team, we played a
game against San Francisco. During the second half, linebacker Charles
Haley hit me pretty hard on the side. I heard a loud snap, and when
I looked down at my ankle, I saw that my foot had turned around
180 degrees and was dangling from my leg. It was my worst injury
yet. The surgery was brutal, but not as painful as the rehab and recovery. Shelly's daily visits and her encouragement and support sustained me. I forced myself to heal and to rebuild the muscles and
stretch the tendons so I could start again the next fall. Unfortunately,
the team hired a new offensive coordinator during that time who
brought in a bunch of new snap plays that I just didn't agree with.
Not only that, but the nature of the plays required a lot of hopping
and sprinting, and I knew that my body just wasn't up for that kind
of action. On the field in my first game with the new coach, we
played against Minnesota. I did what I love to do and called the plays

as I saw them, ignoring the new coach's scripted ones.

If my plays had worked and we had won the game, it would have been all right. I'd have taken some heat, but the head coach Wayne Fontes would have stood behind me. Unfortunately, things didn't go that way. We suffered a dismal loss. Although we were leading for the first three quarters, the Vikings caught on to what we were doing and massacred us. After the game, I said to the head coach, "We need to talk," and he agreed. Never one to draw out the drama, I met with the team management the next day and realized that my career with the Lions was over.

I was given the option to officially "retire," and although my heart would have wanted to play indefinitely, my body and my head had other ideas. It was time to leave and make room for the next up-and-comer. One day I was "Eric Hipple, the NFL quarterback for the Detroit Lions," and the next day, at age 32, I was cut from the team.

As players, we always anticipate that some day we won't be able to continue playing, but this was something I hadn't prepared for mentally. It hurt to not be part of the team anymore. Unlike most guys who retire after 30 or 40 years in other careers, I had 10 years on the job, which is a long career by professional football standards. The following is an article from the *Detroit Free Press:*

● ● ●

Another Tough Break: Hipple is Cut by the Lions[1]

BY CURT SYLVESTER

Free Press Sports Writer (November 8, 1989)

Even tough guys have their limits. And after nearly 10 seasons with the Lions, quarterback Eric Hipple found his. It wasn't the broken ankle in 1988. Or the dislocated thumb in 1987. Or the elbow surgery before that. Or the cracked ribs or sprained knees or broken nose.

But the prospect of spending the rest of his career as a backup quarterback — trying to master an offense he is no longer physically equipped to run — was too much for even Hipple, 32.

He asked to be put on waivers, and Lions coach Wayne Fontes reluctantly agreed Tuesday afternoon.

Other NFL teams have 24 hours to claim him, and Hipple is hoping he'll land with a contender that needs an experienced backup for the stretch drive.

"I'm not ready to retire, not by any means," he said. "I think I've got a lot of playing time left.

"It's just that over the years I've taken a little bit of wear and tear, and I need to be sitting back in the pocket.

"I've got nine years of experience in my head as far as reading defenses. I need to be with a system that can capitalize on it."

When Fontes announced last week he would activate quarterback Chuck Long from injured reserve, there was speculation Hipple might be released.

But it happened the other way. Hipple went to Fontes asking to be released, and Fontes tried to change his mind.

"I tried to talk him out of it," Fontes said. "Eric Hipple has been nothing but class since I've been here. The organization will miss him, the team will miss him, and Wayne Fontes will miss him."

Fontes said Hipple would not have been the player released to make room for Long — back after being on injured reserve since undergoing elbow surgery Feb. 2 — indicating that Fontes intended to cut a player other than a quarterback.

Although he asked to be released, Hipple said he has good feelings toward the Lions and intends to make his home in the Detroit area.

"I feel like I've grown up here," he said. "It's been 10 happy years. There have been some frustrating times, but the happy times by far outweigh the frustrating times."

With Hipple gone, kicker Ed Murray is the senior Lion. Both came into the NFL with the Lions in 1980, Hipple as the fourth-round pick and Murray as the seventh-round pick.

Hipple made his NFL debut as a starter with six touchdowns — four passing, two running — in a Monday night game against the Chicago Bears the next year.

In 1983, Hipple led the Lions to their only division title since 1957. But he suffered a knee injury in the final game of the season and missed the 24-23 playoff loss to San Francisco.

The injury was one of many Hipple suffered during his career, some of which undoubtedly were due to his reckless style of play.

He played with injured ribs and with knees so sore he could hardly hobble. He suffered a broken nose when his helmet was nearly twisted sideways on his head, but continued playing.

Playing in relief of Long against the 49ers last season, Hipple put his shoulder down and slammed into 49ers safety Ronnie Lott when he needed — and got — a first down.

A short time later, 49ers linebacker Charles Haley hit Hipple on a quarterback sack from the blind side, breaking Hipple's ankle with a snap heard all over the field.

While trainers hustled to get him on the stretcher, Hipple talked and joked with 49ers players. He explained later he kept talking to avoid going into shock from the pain.

Hipple felt that if the Lions had stuck to a conventional offense, he might have been able to make a successful comeback. But during training camp, he struggled to pick up the stretch offense.

Nevertheless, he was ready, willing, and eager when Fontes gave him the starting job against Minnesota in the Lions' fifth game of the season.

The results were disastrous. The Vikings' defense hammered Hipple, sacking him five times, intercepting three passes and limiting him to seven completions in 18 attempts for 90 yards.

"I feel fine physically," he said after that game. "Mentally, I couldn't be more upset. I wanted this game so bad, you can't imagine."

Hipple was asked how he would like to be remembered by Lions fans.

"Oh, as a wild kind of guy," he said, laughing. "A scrambler. . . . Really, just as somebody who's given it everything he had. Somebody with a big heart who's fought for everything he's gotten and wasn't afraid to take on a challenge."

How else could it be?

HIPPLE'S CAREER

YEAR	G	ATT/CMP	YDS	TD
1980	15	0/0		
1981	16	279/140	2,358	14
1982	9	86/36	411	2
1983	16	387/204	2,577	12
1984	8	38/16	241	1
1985	16	406/223	2,952	17
1986	16	305/192	1,919	9
1988	5	27/12	158	0
1989	1	18/7	90	0
Total	102	1,546/830	10,706	55

(Hipple spent 1987 on injured reserve because of a thumb injury.)

● ● ●

Even though I had known my playing days would be over at some point, this was a shock. I had no other football options. With all the injuries I'd sustained, I was not what anyone would consider the ideal candidate to be traded. There was so much new talent on the horizon, and other teams didn't relish the idea of having a quarterback past his prime whose future playing ability was uncertain. Although I love the game, life as a coach didn't appeal to me because I didn't want to put my future family or myself through a coach's nomadic life.

Shelly hated to see me leave the game I loved, but she was fully supportive. Jeff and Erica were living with Jann in Utah, and I thought they were young enough not to be affected by the events. I never discussed it with Jann, but I'm sure she was concerned about child support, as I had lost my source of income. Though I had received a severance package, I knew I needed to line up some other jobs to support my family. But before launching a new career, I realized I needed a complete break and some time to think. I bought a camper, and Shelly and I went on a road trip across the country. We explored scenic back roads and colorful towns all across the United States. Shelly and I had been dating for a while by then, and when we reached my home state of California, I proposed to her and she accepted.

Taking the trip with Shelly and getting married created another buzz for me and kept me from feeling the depression of leaving the team. When we returned to Detroit from our cross-country-adventure-turned-honeymoon, I teamed up with some former college players, and we launched an insurance business, HJD, Inc. We worked hard and played hard, and we used our connections and former fame to reel in clients. We would sell insurance as we fished, skied, hunted, and accompanied clients to the Super Bowl. I was a surprisingly effective business manager and was relieved to find that I could develop a stable financial future beyond the NFL. Fox TV invited me to do the local pre-game show, and organizations frequently asked me to make personal appearances at events around the state.

The business went well, and with a buyout of my college friend and his partner, I controlled HJD, Inc. It came to be called Hipple and Associates after adding new partners, and after six years of selling insurance, I was making more than I had from most of my football contracts. Things were going well — maybe too well. Without the thrill of the game and coaches and fans to cheer me on, I slowly became lethargic, bored, and out of shape.

At a former coach's suggestion, I attended several sessions with a psychiatrist, who decided that I was bipolar and wanted to prescribe me a battery of antipsychotic drugs. This just didn't seem like an accurate description of my problem, and I didn't think that after a 10-minute examination a guy could determine I was bipolar. I was pretty familiar with bipolar disorder because one of my cousins had been clinically diagnosed years earlier, and we'd been seeing its effect on her for some time. Later, a friend recommended another psychiatrist, who diagnosed me as having Attention Deficit Hyperactivity Disorder (ADHD). This label was also hard for me to swallow. I'd always had high energy and had been impulsive and pretty spontaneous, but I was able to stay focused when it mattered and didn't really display any of the other classic symptoms. I tried taking the prescribed meds, but they did nothing, so I soon went off them. After that, I self-medicated with a mix of alcohol and prescription painkillers that I always kept readily available to deal with all my football injuries and lethargy.

I soon found myself in a perpetual off-season, with a business that was generating good income but no adrenaline rush. I started to find myself unfocused, tired, and looking for a thrill. However, searching for new adventures, or misadventures, diverted my attention from the business at hand. Taking my eye off the ball proved costly. Our major insurance carrier put a hold on business, and the relationship with my partners deteriorated almost overnight. We became mired in arguments that eventually turned into lawsuits. I learned one important thing: I was not equipped to face this type of adversity. I had always believed in teamwork.

I was miserable. I didn't know how to ask for help or how to describe what I was going through. I just kept trying to put one foot in front of the other and keep our finances afloat. Despite all my efforts, my business was tanking, and I was forced to declare personal bankruptcy. It got so bad that I just knew I could not keep running on the treadmill my life had become.

I had become desperate. One day in 1998 I was on my way to a sales training program in Phoenix, and Shelly was driving me to the airport. I had been hiding feelings of sadness, worthlessness, and helplessness for a while, and I was exhausted. Halfway to the airport, I remember jotting a quick note to Shelly on a napkin reading, "I can't keep doing this," and tossing it in her lap. While the car was zipping down the freeway at 70 miles per hour, I unfastened my seatbelt, opened the passenger door, and jumped out of the car.

I honestly don't know what I was thinking at the time. When I had buckled up at home, I certainly had not planned to attempt suicide. In fact, the idea of even being injured hadn't occurred to me either. I just knew I couldn't go to that meeting and pretend everything was okay. With the mounting problems, my fight-or-flight response had kicked in, and I had no more fight left in me. Flight seemed like a pretty good idea for that split second, and the next thing I knew, I woke up in the hospital emergency room. I had a concussion and a lot of road rash from the pavement, and, by the grace of God, I had no other serious injuries. Looking back on this episode, I can see that I was willing to do anything in my misery to avoid feeling trapped in the darkness of my depression.

Not all times were bad. Because Erica and Jeff spent so much time with us, they really bonded with Shelly and were very close to Taylor and Tarah. I was never happier than when all the kids were with us, and we'd be the loudest, wildest family having fun adventures together. During those wonderful times, I would forget my financial and personal desperation. During those times, I didn't need coaches to give me the plays or fans to cheer me on.

Though Jann and I both tried to maintain composure between us after our divorce, I know that Erica and Jeff paid the price with Jann's subsequent divorce and my personal and business problems. Jeff, in particular, had always done well in school, enjoyed sports, and seemed to enjoy life. But once he reached high school, he found life to be a challenge. In 1995, his mom had just ended her marriage. Jeff had been quite attached to his stepdad, so he felt out of sorts with the situation and started acting out. Jann and I decided to have him come live with me at the end of the school year, as he had done two years earlier.

He took after me and was a good athlete, and he soon became captain of his freshman basketball team. But later, as spring approached, he became lethargic, his grades dropped, and he became ineligible to play for the team he loved. This added just one more burden to his narrow, young shoulders, a burden that would prove more costly than any of us could have imagined. I now know that beyond the external pressures causing his changes, Jeff was trying desperately to cope, as I had, with undiagnosed depression.

I still think of Jeff every day and cherish my wonderful memories of him. One thing I can say is that, unlike his dad, Jeff was always conscious of right and wrong; he would come home from a party rather than drink alcohol. Jann had raised him well, and he was a fine example of what his religion had taught him.

He loved movies, and when *The Blair Witch Project* came out, he didn't venture into our woods as far as he used to on his four-wheeler, until his cousin Jared visited. They were feeling brave and went out one night, and they both came back screaming, swearing they had seen something. What a great imagination!

He was well-coordinated; in addition to playing basketball, he could snow-ski and was just getting good at wakeboarding on Lake Shawnee in Michigan. There really wasn't much Jeff couldn't do. And yes, unfortunately, I had taught him how to use a shotgun. Like so many fathers and sons, we would go skeet shooting together or practice target shooting in the backyard. He knew his way around a firearm.

My son was simply a great kid. He always thought of others and what could bring a smile to your face. He was a talented impersonator and could imitate Jim Carrey wonderfully, often entertaining us with clips from movies like *The Mask* or *Liar, Liar*. His dancing imitations of Carlton (from the TV show *The Fresh Prince of Bel Air*) would always bust us up. In addition to being a good actor, Jeff was artistic. He was meticulous about his drawings, paying attention to every little detail.

Jeff was fast, agile, and handsome, but not without his quirks. He always wore two pairs of socks and didn't like grass on his bare feet. He was known as "Birdie" by his friends, both for the bird noises he could make and because of his bird-like legs. He was always thoughtful of his sisters. He would get down with his younger sisters and play at their level, and he would play at his older sister's level by being the doting or nagging brother. Jeff's demeanor made it easy for him to make friends, yet due to his depression, I don't think he knew how special he really was.

It's hard to write about Jeff. Just like that old cliché, you don't truly realize how special someone is until he is gone. Though I was one to say, "I love you" and was not afraid of showing emotion like my father was, I fear I still came up short.

In early April 2000, in what came to be remembered as Jeff's final days, he was living with us in Michigan. Jeff was looking forward to spending time with his sister Erica, who was just starting her senior year of high school in Salt Lake City. She was contemplating future college plans and excited to spend time with Jeff over the coming spring break.

This was a bad time for me, as I was struggling with my two business partners, who were preparing to sue me in a dispute we easily could have resolved over a cup of coffee. I was stressed and concerned about Jeff's continuing lethargy, but I had to fly to Canada for business reasons. Jeff stayed home with Shelly and the girls, and I remember kissing him goodbye and reassuring him that he'd be visiting his mom in a week. Little did I know, this would be the last time I'd see my beautiful boy alive.

While in Canada, I stayed with some friends and business associates in their house at Whistler Ski Resort. The day after I arrived, my friend Tibor Gyarmati received a call from Shelly. I'll never forget the stunned look on Tibor's face as he listened on the telephone. He handed me the phone and said softly, "Jeff is dead."

I said, "That's not even a funny joke."

As he held the phone out to me, Tibor said, "I'm not joking."

Every muscle in my body tightened as I asked Shelly, "What's going on?"

I'll never forget hearing her tearful words: "Jeff is gone." Those words are forever singed into my memory.

I literally have no recollection of returning to Michigan from Canada — I was in total shock. My colleagues somehow got me on the last flight back to Michigan that night, and I returned home in the early morning hours. I wanted to scream to everyone on the flight, "How can you just sit there when Jeff is dead?"

Over and over I asked myself how this gorgeous 15-year-old could be dead. How could he have been in so much pain I couldn't see? How could he be alive when I kissed him goodbye, and be dead now? It was beyond my comprehension.

I was driven home in a fog, like a surreal dream. It couldn't be real. As we drove up to the house, Shelly and the girls surrounded me. We screamed and cried all in one huddle. I needed to get the details. How could I make sense of the senseless? Shelly sat me down and tried to explain the inexplicable.

While Shelly had been out grocery shopping, Jeff was at home babysitting our youngest daughter Tarah and her friend. He had set them up with some snacks and a video in front of the television, then had gone to the master bedroom, retrieved my hunting rifle from under the bed, and loaded it with a shell he had stashed away. Jeff then had gone into the master bathroom, removed his shoes and socks, put his big toe in the trigger, and shot himself in the head. When Shelly walked in the front door with the groceries, Tarah told her she'd just heard a loud noise like a gun. Shelly ran to the bedroom to check. As she entered the bedroom, she saw only Jeff's legs sticking out of the bathroom door, completely still. The realization hit her, and she knew he was dead. She ran to the neighbors' house, and they called the police. Then Shelly called me in Canada.

As Shelly recounted the story, all I could think was, "Oh God, how could this have happened?" I was beyond devastated. We all were in shock and couldn't believe that Jeff was dead and wouldn't be coming through the door within a couple minutes. We all expected that he'd soon bring his grades back up and resume his high school sports. We all thought he had so much to live for.

Chapter Six

Monday Morning Quarterbacking

What had gone wrong? Had there been warning signs all along that I somehow just hadn't seen? Using 20/20 hindsight, I now understand that Jeff had been calling out for help for some time, but I just hadn't known enough to comprehend what was going on with him. How could I have when I didn't recognize the symptoms in myself?

They say there are no better "Monday morning quarterbacks" than actual seasoned quarterbacks who have called plans, passed, run, been tackled, and gotten back up too many times to count. That being the case, I hope you'll forgive me if I interject a bit of this hindsight bias into my own life. Looking back through the prism of memories with the knowledge I have since gained as the University of Michigan Depression Center outreach program coordinator, I'd say that the younger Eric, like Jeff, had displayed some pretty clear signs of depression: negative thinking, loss of energy, profound sadness, substance abuse. Experts say depression is often hard to detect, especially in boys, and especially in boys who appear successful in most everything they do (like those who excel in sports).

I now can see some family history and signs of depression. My mom's "quiet spells" were probably some pretty deep bouts. We also have some family history of depression and mental illness, which I now recognize as going hand-in-hand. One of my aunts has been diagnosed with schizophrenia and my sister's daughter has a clinical diagnosis of bipolar disorder. I came from a family where depression was omnipresent, yet it was never recognized, let alone openly discussed. Quite the contrary, I was told early on to "act like a man." This carried over to my undiagnosed depression after my forced retirement from the Lions. I don't ever want to ignore mental illness or depression again. I want us all to be quarterbacks, not "Monday morning quarterbacks." I want to yell at the world, "Stop the play! Pay attention — life is happening!" I realize the signs and symptoms of depression now, too late for Jeff, but not for my girls. Also, I want to share my experience with you.

I know that, like Jeff, depressed teens exhibiting symptoms often don't have a clue about what's wrong; they just "don't feel good." Children may take excessive numbers of sick days from school, or they may have insomnia or just want to sleep all the time, as Jeff and I did. Look for dramatic changes in appetite and mood swings. Sometimes depressed teens will cry privately, but due to societal stigma against men shedding any tears, this is often difficult to detect in boys. I still ask myself why I didn't see these signs.

I remember one day during Jeff's final year when I took him to see his pediatrician. He said he just hadn't been feeling well, and he hadn't been hungry at all. I told the doctor that I'd had to pry Jeff out of bed just to get him to the appointment that morning. Even the doctor didn't see it as depression; he just attributed it to a mild virus and said things would get better.

Looking back, I want to scream.

Why didn't I know? Why couldn't even the doctor diagnose such clear-cut symptoms? I can't help but think that if just one person in Jeff's life had known the symptoms of depression, he would be alive today.

I'm not trying to say that brief bouts of the blues are abnormal. Certainly every teenager goes through periods of angst and confusion, especially when triggered by events like failing a class, breaking up with a girlfriend, parents' divorce, hormones, or having to move midway through high school. These all cause stress and would rightfully make anyone feel bad. What I'm talking about are symptoms like Jeff's: longer periods of feeling you're under a very dark cloud, of feeling hopeless and worthless, like the light at the end of the tunnel is a train coming toward you.

If I had only had the University of Michigan's brief diagnostic questions, I would have known Jeff was tending toward depression. Why is it important to know this? Because once a medical professional diagnoses depression, you need to get help — the help that Jeff never received and I didn't get until it was too late. This is why, before I go any further with my story, I want you to have this knowledge before it's too late for you or someone you love.

Following are the symptoms I didn't recognize in myself or in Jeff. If any of these apply to you, grab a pencil, and jot down your responses. If you think someone you know may be depressed, consider asking him or her to take this test. Also encourage him or her to read the "Asking for Help" section on page 55.

❖ ❖ ❖

Nine-Symptom Checklist for Depression[2]

For each of the statements below, insert the following scores for your responses:

> 0 = Never/not at all
> 1 = Several days
> 2 = More than half the days
> 3 = Nearly every day

Over the last two weeks, how often have you experienced or been bothered by any of the following:

a. Little interest or pleasure in doing things _____

b. Feeling down, depressed, or hopeless _____

c. Trouble falling asleep, staying asleep, or sleeping too much _____

d. Feeling tired or having little energy _____

e. Poor appetite or overeating _____

f. Feeling bad about yourself, feeling that you are a failure, or feeling that you have let yourself or a loved one down _____

g. Trouble concentrating on things such as reading or watching television _____

h. Moving or speaking so slowly that other people could have noticed, or being so fidgety or restless that you move around a lot more than usual _____

i. Thinking that you would be better off dead or that you want to hurt yourself in some way _____

If you scored 1 or more for any of the above statements so far, how difficult have these problems made it for you to do your work, take care of things at home, or perform at school?

0 = Not Difficult at All   1 = Somewhat Difficult
2 = Very Difficult   3 = Extremely Difficult _____

TOTAL SCORE _____

Interpreting Your Score — How to Determine When You Might Need Help

Your total score of:	*Might indicate that you:*
4 or less	May be experiencing tough times but may not need professional treatment
5 to 14	Should consider speaking with a professional: your doctor, a counselor, therapist, or other mental health specialist
15 or more	May be experiencing clinical depression and likely would benefit from a thorough checkup and possibly antidepressant medication and therapy

● ● ●

Asking for Help

You now know the nine symptoms of depression, and you have become what I couldn't be for Jeff: educated. Use your knowledge to take control of the situation. You need not be a victim held hostage by the ignorance or apathy of the overworked health care system. Find some degree of professional help, which can be especially difficult if you are already feeling down like Jeff and can't express what you're feeling.

This is why I want you to take your completed checklist with you when you visit your doctor. Be careful! Depending on your score, you may need immediate help. If so, make an appointment with your primary care physician *now!* Don't wait. Your doctor will also want to rule out any potential physical causes for how you're feeling. Depression often shares symptoms with other illnesses, and you want to be sure you're not overlooking another serious illness. Once your physician has ruled out or treated any other physical ailments, ask him or her to refer you to a mental health professional who specializes in depression.

Don't panic. You're not crazy. These folks specialize in treating illnesses like depression, and you really can benefit from the options available now.

The important thing to know — and, in hindsight, what I wish I'd known then — is that *depression is treatable.* It is an illness, and you no longer have to feel awful all the time. A variety of treatments really do work, and you *can* feel better. You can feel like yourself again. There is hope for a brighter tomorrow. I promise. I think that had I been treated way back in high school, I would have been better able to weather the highs and lows of the roller coaster ride that was my life after high school, and I would have recognized the symptoms in Jeff.

At this point, I want to share with you some of the things I've learned about depression and suicide since Jeff ended his life. I've learned these signs of suicide risk through my affiliation with the doctors at the University of Michigan Depression Center. I will comment on a few of the signs that I now know Jeff experienced. Even though it is too late to save Jeff's life, I'm hoping this information might save someone else. Jeff exhibited most of these signs; we just didn't know what they meant. Keep in mind that not everyone with depression will attempt suicide, but if the signs seem familiar, please err on the side of caution and get help.

■ ■ ●

Signs Of Depression and Possible Suicide Risk[3]

Talking About Dying — any mention of dying, disappearing, jumping, shooting oneself, or other types of self-harm

Jeff had been talking about suicide with a girlfriend from school. We found their notes later.

Recent Loss — through death, divorce, separation, broken relationship, loss of job, money, status, self-confidence, self-esteem, loss of religious faith, loss of interest in friends, sex, hobbies, or previously enjoyed activities

Jeff's losses included the position of basketball team captain and the divorce of his mother and stepfather, as well as my depression and failing business.

Change in Personality — sadness, withdrawal, irritability, anxiety, tiredness, indecisiveness, apathy

Jeff showed all of these moods.

Change in Behavior — inability to concentrate on school, work, routine tasks

Jeff's grades had dropped below a C average.

Change in Sleep Patterns — insomnia, often with early waking or oversleeping, nightmares

Jeff had difficulty sleeping and would oversleep during the day.

Change in Eating Habits — loss of appetite and weight, or overeating

Jeff just didn't seem hungry and had lost weight.

Diminished Sexual Interest — impotence or menstrual abnormalities (often missed periods)

Fear of Losing Control — fear of going crazy, harming self or others

Low Self-Esteem — feelings of worthlessness, shame, overwhelming guilt, self-hatred; thinking, "everyone would be better off without me"

Jeff had been feeling like he didn't belong. When he was with me, he wanted to be with Jann, and vice versa.

No Hope for the Future — belief that things will never get better, that nothing will ever change

Jeff must have felt very strongly that things would never improve if he had planned to shoot himself.

Other Symptoms — suicidal impulses, statements, or plans; giving away favorite things; previous suicide attempts; substance abuse; making out wills; arranging for the care of pets; extravagant spending; agitation; hyperactivity; restlessness or lethargy

REMEMBER:
The risk of suicide may be greatest as the depression lifts, because the sufferer regains enough energy to act on self-destructive thoughts.

● ● ●

Sometimes, especially if a person has been feeling down for a while as Jeff had been, he or she may feel tempted to just end it all. Some people may feel like putting themselves in harm's way or killing themselves. If you feel this way or are aware of a friend or loved one who has been having these thoughts, I hope you will accept my advice and seek help right away. You may feel foolish asking a loved one or friend if he or she is suicidal, but it's better to get these feelings out in the open than risk the loss of a very precious life.

● ● ●

57

Get Help Immediately

The National Institute of Mental Health offers the following resources if you are thinking about suicide. **Bottom line: Get help immediately.**

- Call your doctor's office. I went to the doctor with Jeff, but none of us recognized the signs. Make sure your doctor understands depression. If you are uncertain, get a second opinion.

- Call 911 for emergency services. Go to the emergency room of the nearest hospital.

- Ask a family member or friend to call your doctor or take you to the hospital.

- Call the toll-free, 24-hour hotline of the National Suicide Prevention Lifeline at 1-800-273-TALK (1-800-273-8255) to be connected to a trained counselor at the suicide crisis center nearest you.[4]

● ● ●

Thank you for learning these signs. Having this information could save your own life or the life of a loved one. I do not want one more person to experience the heartache I felt after Jeff's death. Nothing could have prepared me. It was hell. I didn't know how I was going to survive the pain or whether I even wanted to. I had so many unanswered — and unanswerable — questions. Why did he do it? Why wasn't I there? Could I have stopped it? Why didn't I get rid of my shotgun? Where did Jeff get the bullet? The overwhelming feeling I endured was sheer pain. I cried more during those first six months after losing him than ever in my life. The tears often would come unexpectedly — I'd hear a song that Jeff had loved by Green Day or Creed; I'd see the Jeep he'd always dreamed of driving; we'd get a call from one of his friends. It was just too much for me to handle, and the tears would flow. I know that I must have wigged out a few people. Here was this big, rugged former NFL quarterback sobbing like a baby, or at times just blubbering uncontrollably. The tears were there, and at that point I didn't give a damn what people thought. I was so sad, and the grief was profound.

Of course, the local news and papers were filled with headlines of "NFL Detroit Lions Quarterback Eric Hipple's Son Dies by Suicide." We held a service at Jeff's high school at the principal's request. Because I was a high-profile member of the community, the principal felt that it would be important for the student body. I don't know how I knew to do it, but I found some printed material on suicide, made a flyer on suicide risk factors, and passed it out to the students.

Today, I think what we coordinated was not so much a funeral as it was a "suicide prevention assembly," except Jeff's casket was there with his picture on it. Erica read a poem, and Jann and I spoke. I said that Jeff was not a hero, but had a mental illness. I said that taking your life is never an option. The school was highly grateful. They recorded the entire session, and I must say it was very painful. After eight years, I look at the tape of two deeply bereaved parents and Jeff's siblings, and I wonder how we ever did it. I would never suggest that any family do what we did, but who knows — it may have saved another life. We held a private memorial service attended by more than 1,000 people — it was overwhelming. We then went on to Logan, Utah, where we held a second service, again attended by a huge crowd. Out of the goodness of her heart, Jann paid for the funeral arrangements and our airline tickets, as I was still experiencing financial difficulties.

The shame and guilt I felt over the suicide was intense. I was sure everyone was blaming our family and trying to find where we had gone wrong. The girls were all confused, wondering whether they had said or done something that had caused Jeff to give up. I also felt angry with Jeff. How could he do this to our family? Jann's family blamed me. My family blamed Jann. I blamed myself. We had enough blame to fill the Silverdome Stadium. In the end, no one was to blame — Jeff had a disease, and this disease is called "depression."

After the funerals and assembly, I had a major life meltdown and was unable to work or even show up for an event. In some ways, it felt good to sort out the many feelings and emotions. Some of these were directly related to grief, and I now know they were a normal part of the grieving process. Feelings would hit me randomly, or sometimes all at once. The grief came in unexpected waves and pounded me like a fierce ocean storm. I felt guilty. I felt scared. I felt angry. I felt numb. I felt stressed. And I felt lonely. My neck was stiff from straining to find that beautiful blond head in crowds. But guilt was the strongest emotion. Why hadn't I been there? I should have been able to see it coming. I should have stopped it.

I also suffered what is called "survivor's guilt." If someone had to die, why not me, who already had lived a pretty full life? Why Jeff, who wasn't even through his teen years? Since I've been involved with the University of Michigan's study on men and depression, I have learned a lot that has helped my brain come to terms with what happened. Initially nobody could have convinced me that I ever would heal from the intense pain I was feeling, but more than eight years have passed now. Although my heart still feels the loss, my pain is not as intense, and I am slowly finding joy again.

Jann and Shelly, as well as our three daughters, Erica, Taylor, and Tarah, have shared the pain. Seeing them grieve has been tough. Members of our larger family circle tried to offer as much support as they could, but they, too, were grieving. We just couldn't get over the fact that Jeff had killed himself and how senseless his death seemed. I know Jann felt guilty for not keeping him in Utah. She wondered whether a different decision would have saved his life.

Shelly and I felt sick with guilt over the fact that we hadn't recognized any symptoms during our time with Jeff, and I felt absolutely horrible that he had used my own shotgun as the weapon. I had always taught my children about the danger of firearms, and I thought that my own had been safely put away. However, Jeff had apparently found the hidden ammunition and the rifle under my bed — the weapon of his ultimate destruction. Jeff's suicide was something I would have to live with for the rest of my life, and this realization ate me up inside. I would ultimately have to find a way to forgive myself, or I would destroy everything important left in my life.

The support we received from former coaches and teammates truly humbled me. I saw a side of them I never had seen before. To have these big guys come listen to me and cry with me was incredibly moving. They, as well as friends from our neighborhood, business, and church, surrounded us and took care of us all for a while. Sometimes it was most helpful just to have someone over who'd sit and not need to talk, just be there with us. When we would talk about Jeff and cry together, we felt less isolated, less alone. I know I was in a daze during that time, and I hope that those kind-hearted folks know how much we appreciated the support and love they shared with us during the most difficult time of our lives. I don't know how I would have survived without them.

In addition to dealing with my own grief, we were also dealing with the grief of Erica, Taylor, and Tarah. They had lost their only brother, someone they adored. This absolutely devastated them.

I didn't really understand how much Jeff's sisters were suffering until Dr. Heidi Horsley interviewed the family for this book and talked with us about the loss of her brother, Scott, as the result of an auto accident in 1983. Heidi noted that sibling death in childhood is a rare event having profound effects on surviving siblings. It is an event that should not happen.[5] Our siblings are the ones who take life's journey with us; they know things about us that nobody else knows. So, when we lose a brother or sister, in a sense we lose part of our history. Heidi pointed out that our relationship with our siblings is supposed to last from 80 to 100 percent of our life spans.[6]

The girls really identified with Heidi when she said that Scott's death rocked her world and put everything she ever believed into question. Each sister experienced Jeff's death differently, based on her age and her relationship with him; Erica was 18, Taylor was nine, and Tarah was seven. Jeff's death by his own hand made the loss even more frightening for them. The girls felt that Jeff had chosen death over life with them. In addition to the typical emotions of grief, Jeff's siblings had to deal with the stigma of suicide. They felt that our family had been placed under a microscope. What really had gone on with this family behind closed doors? As if we weren't feeling enough guilt ourselves. This stigma left the sisters feeling disconnected, not only from support, but also, at times more profoundly, from God.

If these feelings sound familiar to you or your children, you might want to consider reading Dr. Gloria Horsley and Dr. Heidi Horsley's book, *Teen Grief Relief.* It contains many tips to help teens, and I recommend it highly. One of the most important things I've learned from Jeff's death is that you have to be honest about what happened in order to help children deal with suicide. The children needed to know how Jeff had died, especially Erica, who had not been there at the time. Otherwise, there is a skeleton in the closet, and no matter how tightly you shut the door, eventually children will learn the truth or maybe even fabricate stories to explain the death. Our counselors advised us to disclose as much as necessary so the girls could understand what had happened. I wanted to be honest with our children because I knew they would suffer even more if they sensed they were being lied to. Not only would they suffer from the loss of their brother, but they also would lose trust in me. I did not want to increase their feelings of isolation because of this mysterious, deep, dark secret nobody talks about.

I've noticed that my children tend to ask about what they need to know, so Shelly and I have tried to answer them. I've learned that total honesty — disclosure of all the facts — takes a lot less energy than trying to edit the story about the end of someone's life. Honesty sometimes elicits unwittingly cruel comments or observations from others, such as from one of Jann's relatives who screamed at me, "What the *hell* was a *gun* doing in your house anyway?"

The girls also wondered if they were somehow to blame for Jeff's suicide. Shelly and I tried to reassure them that Jeff had made his own decision, and it had nothing to do with them. We also learned that the girls had developed fears that they too would die, or that Shelly, other surviving relatives, or I might die or commit suicide. After Jeff's death, Taylor and Tarah often became extremely anxious and agitated if Shelly and I were late getting home, afraid that something had happened to us. We felt the same fear if they were late. Tarah recently told me she still panics if a friend or her sister isn't right on time. This is a sad example of how grief changes a world view forever. Our family has made an anti-suicide pact and an agreement that we will talk with each other about our feelings — we don't ever want suicide to impact our family again.

After the shock of Jeff's suicide, I spent my energy just trying to survive. One lesson I've learned the hard way is to not compare my own loss with other people's losses. I have found that we all experience grief in our own way. Well-meaning (yet totally insensitive) people would say the stupidest things, like, "Well, at least it was fast, not like so-and-so, who slowly suffocated while hanging." Or others, who told us, "I know *exactly* how you feel. When my sister died from prolonged lung cancer, I felt the same way." Or, "At least you could always have another son — I'll never have another husband like Stan."

After talking with hundreds of people, I have found that each loss has its own meaning, and we each have our own unique collection of coping skills and experience that determines how we will heal.

Dr. Robert Neimeyer, a professor at the University of Memphis and author of many books, including *Meaning Reconstruction and the Experience of Loss,*[7] lost his father to suicide when he was just 11 years old. Dr. Neimeyer recognizes that after a death, we often must seek and find new meaning in our own lives. So after a loss, how do we create this new meaning? According to Dr. Neimeyer, each person does this uniquely. Some create new meaning quietly through personal prayer and journaling. Others may move into action by advocating for change, carrying on some of the charitable work the deceased did, or starting a foundation in memory of their loved one.

Although I won't compare the grief that death by suicide brings with the grief from other types of death, I will say that overcoming suicide grief can be more complicated because of the stigma of suicide, the guilt, and the number of unanswered questions. My family needed to accept that we would never "get over it," but we could get through it. We found that we needed to own our feelings, reach out to others, and acknowledge the reality of the situation. It was our way of working through the pain.

Some of the lessons I've learned may seem like common sense to others, but we were totally clueless at the time. We didn't know about suicide warning signs, suicide prevention, and what is called "suicide postvention," or tools for coping with the aftermath of a suicide. I think it's important to share these ideas with you, and I hope you will pay close attention to these warning signs, as they may help save a life. If you want to skip ahead to continue my story, feel free.

● ● ●

Do Not Be Afraid to Ask...

The information that follows comes from various sources, which I cite in the "Resources" section at the end of this book. Thanks especially to the National Institute of Mental Health, the University of Michigan Depression Center,[8] and the San Francisco Suicide Prevention Hotline.[9]

DO NOT BE AFRAID TO ASK:

"Do you sometimes feel so bad you think of suicide?"

> Just about everyone has considered suicide, however fleetingly, at one time or another. There is no danger of "giving someone the idea." In fact, it can be a great relief if you bring the questions of suicide into the open and discuss them freely without showing shock or disapproval. Raising the question of suicide shows that you are taking the person seriously and responding to his or her distress.

If the answer is: *"Yes. I do think of suicide."*

You must take it seriously and follow through.

"Have you thought how you'd do it?" "Do you have a plan?" "Do you have the means?" "Have you decided when you would do it?" "Have you ever tried suicide before?" "What happened then?"

> If the person has a definite plan, if the means are easily available, or if the method is a lethal one and the time is set, the risk of suicide is very high. You will gear your responses to the urgency of the situation as you see it. Therefore, it is vital not to underestimate the danger by not asking for the details.

REMEMBER:
Always ask "How?" and "When?" before "Why?"
These questions tell you the first signs of serious risk.
You determine the degree of suicide risk further by applying the
criteria outlined in: "Evaluating Suicide Risk," on the next page.

Making A Contract: If you conclude that the risk of suicide is high (i.e., a strong possibility exists that the person will die by suicide in the near future), try to make a verbal agreement with the person to contact you before he or she follows through with suicidal intentions.

* * *

Evaluating Suicide Risk

Things to watch for when assessing potential suicide risk include:

Plan — Does the person have one?

Obviously, Jeff did.

Lethality — Is it lethal? Can they die?

A firearm always has the possibility of being lethal.

Availability — Does the person have the means to carry out the plan?

Unfortunately, I kept my shotgun in our house.

Illness — Do they have a mental or physical illness?

Our family history included my aunt's and niece's mental illnesses. I now know that I suffered from depression, as well.

Depression — Chronic or specific incident(s)?

Jeff had been showing signs of depression; drop in grades, apathy, sleep problems, somatic pains, low self-esteem, irritability, withdrawal from friends.

Previous Attempts — How many? How recent?

Jeff had none that we knew of.

Alone — Is the person alone? Does he or she have a support system? A partner? Is the person alone right now?

Jeff had been missing his mom and his stepfather.

Loss — Has the person suffered a loss? Death, job, relationship, self-esteem?

Jeff's school had taken him off the basketball team due to his dropped grade point average, and he had experienced the loss of his stepdad due to divorce.

Substance Abuse (or Use) — Drugs, alcohol, medicine? Current, chronic?

None. As a practicing Mormon, Jeff did not use drugs or alcohol.

● ● ●

I hope these comments and this assessment will help you. I so regret not knowing then what I have learned in the time since Jeff died. If I had, perhaps he would still be with us. Perhaps I also could have avoided many painful years of depression, self-medication, and unhealthy behavior.

Chapter Seven

Numbing the Pain, Then Crashing, Then Burning

When I speak about my experiences of loss, some people ask me what I think the differences are between grief and depression. I tell them that they may seem similar on the surface, but I've found that the emotions and feelings of grief tend to come in waves. Somehow I would feel like I was healing one day, and the next day I would sink into despair, bereft of that bright light that had once been part of me. On another day, I would feel denial; I would wake up forgetting that Jeff was gone, thinking it had all just been a bad dream, and then the sudden realization of his death would just crush me. I would cry, go for a drive, or veg out. The feeling eventually subsided, and then I'd be on to the next wave. Unlike the passing, cyclic nature of my grief feelings, once the gloom of depression settled in, it stayed. I felt totally hopeless, helpless, and worthless, and a sense of doom pervaded me without respite.

I also displayed physical aspects of grief. For me, grief affected my sleep patterns — I just never felt fully rested, and my mind would race all night, going over "what ifs?" I also lost my appetite, and my previously formidable immune system left me open to an onslaught of colds, digestive problems, and allergies. Grief also affected my sex drive — I felt so numb inside and at times couldn't bear to be touched; yet at other times I craved physical intimacy just to feel alive again. I've learned that these aspects of grief are pretty normal. Other people sometimes lose their sense of taste, feel exhausted, and often feel that grief has short-circuited their body's electrical system. This can lead to lapses in memory, disorientation (especially forgetting other people's names and mixing up calendar appointments), and a sense of vulnerability and stiffness.

When I was depressed, I had many of the same grief symptoms, but they were combined with feelings of hopelessness and loss of self-worth. I think the unrelenting endurance of symptoms differentiates depression from grief. With depression, sufferers typically feel that all light and hope have been extinguished and that there is no purpose in struggling against all odds any longer. Even before Jeff's suicide, I found that my depression could last for several days or several months. Ultimately, it was many years before I finally got treatment. When I was depressed, I experienced physical pain that felt like general malaise — it was hard to pinpoint exactly where it was coming from, but there was always a sense of just not feeling well.

Fortunately, with grief came numbness and denial, which lingered until I was strong enough to deal with Jeff's death and slowly begin the healing process. I truly believe that if I had been forced to feel the full intensity of the pain all at once, I would have died from the agony. Jeff's death came on top of many other previously mentioned stressors in my life: my forced retirement from football, the failure of my business, financial stress, recurring pain, and surgery for past football injuries. The combination of them all ultimately threw me into a deep depression that went beyond the normal grief symptoms, and at times I felt I would never escape. The initial numbness eventually wore off a few months after Jeff died, and the grim reality of life without him set in. At that point, the pain was just too much to bear, so I turned to alcohol and prescription painkillers to mask the heartache and enable me to just get through the day. I was in a deep, dark funk, and the only way I could function was to drink all day long. Being constantly buzzed like this was not good, and it seriously clouded my judgment. Even though I didn't realize this at the time, it also meant I was just not dealing with my grief. I knew only that I was miserable beyond belief.

The depression wasn't new. When I leaped out of the moving car, the doctors treated my physical injuries and sent me home. People actually made a joke of my jumping out of the car, chuckling, "Oh, that's Eric!" Amazingly enough, none of the doctors who treated me after the accident asked any of the questions that easily would have indicated a diagnosis of depression. Even if they had just asked if I was experiencing any of the acknowledged life stressors, they would have discovered that I was at risk for a stress breakdown or depression. If the doctors had given me more information, I may have been able to recognize the symptoms in my son later.

My life stressors have included various events that alter the course of someone's life. Some examples of life stressors are divorce, separation from family, death of a family member or close friend, physical or mental abuse, and change in financial status. These do not necessarily cause depression, but sometimes one or more of these can be the proverbial straw that breaks the camel's back and launches us into a full-scale depression. For me, Jeff's death was that final straw. I now believe that at various times in my life since my early teen years, I likely have been deeply depressed. I just didn't know it, nor did I know that it was not normal to feel that way for extended stretches of time.

Talking with former NFL athletes and participants in the Men's Depression Center, I've learned several risk factors that could trigger depression in boys and men. The following triggered my depression. Do any of them look familiar? Acknowledging these triggers and modifying my behavior helped me when I began to feel stressed. I hope acknowledging these risk factors will help you.

● ● ●

Triggers of Depression in Men and Boys

Loss of job through layoff or retirement

Loss of physical ability forced me to retire.

Financial setbacks that put the family's lifestyle at risk

The insurance business was going bankrupt, and I faced a series of lawsuits.

Ongoing health problems such as diabetes, injuries, cancer, or heart disease

Numerous football injuries caused me chronic pain and discomfort.

Divorce

My first marriage ended in divorce, and I was worried that Shelly would give up on me.

Excessive alcohol or drug use

I was trying to kill my pain and feelings of distress with drugs and alcohol. I had abused alcohol periodically since my early teens.

Significant debt load and the sense that you'll never get out from under it

I had to file for bankruptcy.

● ● ●

Over the following few years, I cycled through bouts of deep depression that alternated with periods of feeling relatively fine. When

I was feeling fine, I'd still drink socially, especially when I got together with my former teammates or football fans at tailgate parties and post-game celebrations. After Jeff died, all the drinking and self-medication didn't just numb the pain, it also postponed any healing. I was oblivious and just knew I couldn't get through the long days and sleepless nights without help.

* * *

So, I've already described how I went from Monday Night Football to Monday night in jail and how I eventually ended up serving a 58-day sentence because I just couldn't bring myself to conform to the judge's requirements. I was in jail with some guys who'd been in and out many times over the years. A lot of them blamed others for their situations. They never held themselves accountable or responsible for any of their actions, any of their crimes, or any of the horrors their victims suffered. I realized that, to a certain degree, I had been thinking the same way when I went in. After several weeks in lockup, I experienced a big turnaround moment realizing that I needed to examine my life and actions, and take responsibility. The content of the group therapy sessions in jail didn't help me, but I found them beneficial because they pointed out that some guys just never get it, and I didn't want to be one of those guys. Learning from mistakes isn't always the easiest thing to do, but some of the guys in jail just never learned. They came in and out, over and over again, and they always blamed others for their incarceration.

Although it was not technically therapeutic, spending time in jail did give me a lot of time to think, to really contemplate. My most powerful realization came when I tried to answer questions for myself. How had I gotten to this point in my life? How had I let this happen? I had just lost my son, and now I was going to screw up my life and lose my family and likely everything else. I felt great sorrow, a lot of sadness, and shame. I knew that I could do better. I was ashamed at what my family, Shelly's parents, and Jann's family all thought about what I'd done. I realized that *I needed to change my thinking and behavior,* and that was probably the hardest-won realization. According to Dr. Robert Holden, bestselling author and founder of "The Happiness Project," you must first decide to be happy before you can take the actual steps to achieve happiness.

Up to that point, I still had been trying to assert my own authority, my own will. I had not been willing to cooperate and just go along with the judge's program and learn. I kept thinking I could beat the system and make my own kind of deal, that I somehow could get around the obstacles the criminal justice system kept putting in my way.

Going to jail reminded me of getting benched during a game. You sit and watch everybody else run the plays and receive the fans' applause, and you suddenly realize, "Gee, the fans don't like me anymore, and I'm getting booed and sitting out on all the fun." The irony wasn't lost on me; I was aware of the stark contrast. I would see that Monday Night Football game, the one in which I set records and had made the best debut. I would see the toughest Lions quarterback, ranked fifth in all-time passing, then I would fast forward to seeing the flashing police lights, being pulled over, and knowing I'd had too much to drink. My dad had attended every one of my games, and I thought about his disappointment when he heard of my arrest. I think the shame hurt most of all.

I have learned that we each form just part of a much bigger picture. We can control only what we are able to control: our reactions, our thoughts, and our deeds. We cannot control or force an outcome that doesn't belong to us. We have the right to our work, but the results are out of our hands.

Again, as I said at the beginning of the book, getting arrested was probably the best thing that could have happened to me. I didn't realize it at the time, but I definitely had spun out of control. I simply didn't care, and I was trying to stay as numb as possible. An overriding darkness pervaded my soul. My jail term served as an automatic 58-day detox program as well, so I also could attribute my growing clarity to the lack of alcohol or medications in my system. According to the Department of Health and Human Services (2006), men are more likely to drink excessively than women. In fact, roughly 65 percent of men reported drinking within the past 30 days and were three times more likely to binge drink. In addition, approximately 20 percent of all males will become alcohol dependent during their lifetime. As you can see, I was right on target.

I still find it hard to believe that through all those years I never had become even remotely aware of depression's symptoms or the likelihood that I had being facing it since my teenage years. As I looked back at my life, I could see that Jeff had been experiencing many of the same feelings and issues I'd faced at his age. My time in jail prepared me for a drastic life change that would have lasting effects.

Chapter 8

Making a Comeback

a few months after my release from jail — about a year and a half after Jeff's death — the University of Michigan Center for Depression invited me to be part of a Lunch & Learn session. After the lunch, I ended up speaking with some of the doctors leading the studies there, and I mentioned some of the issues I'd been facing. The doctors referred me to Dr. Ribiero, a great doctor at the Center, and, after a thorough analysis, I received my first diagnosis of agitated depression. Amazingly, also for the first time, my doctor and I discussed all the symptoms and what they meant. We explored all the options for treatment together, including the pros and cons of each. With my previous diagnoses of bipolar disorder and ADHD, the doctors simply had handed me a stack of prescriptions and said "do this" or "do that," without explaining what was physically happening to me and why. Maybe I didn't feel ready to hear it. Perhaps this sounds familiar to some of you.

This was the first instance anyone took the time to explain how the brain's chemistry works, that depression is a physical illness that throws the brain's chemistry out of whack. Together, we decided the best approach for me would be a combination of medications and cognitive behavioral therapy (CBT). CBT teaches you how the brain works, what the triggers for depression are, how to avoid or mitigate them, and how to use specific clinically-proven techniques. (A fuller description of these techniques appears at the end of this chapter.) In addition, CBT included traditional therapy sessions with a professional to whom I felt comfortable disclosing my life, warts and all. We also discussed my family history of depression, which helped verify that I'd been suffering from it since childhood. This discussion also revealed that my mom likely had been suffering in silence for much of her life.

Initially, Dr. Ribiero started me on some antidepressant and anti-anxiety medication, and he warned me that we might need to experiment a bit to find the ideal medication and dosage for my illness. He was right. We tried different dosages and augmentations before we hit the right combination. The heavy, dark cloud of depression that had engulfed me lifted. The air smelled sweeter, colors shone more vividly, and I felt lighter. The combination of therapy and medication worked well for me, and I finally began to feel again that life was actually worth living. I continue to take the medication today, and it is a small price to pay for my sense of well-being.

Once you have found the right combination of medications for you, whether they be sleep medication, mood stabilizers, or antidepressants, it is extremely important to stay with it. There were and are times that my medications keep me alive from day to day. This doesn't mean you have to take the medications for a lifetime, especially for young people, but it does mean you need ongoing evaluation and support from your doctor. Not until I got serious and adhered to my prescribed medication regimen did I get my life back and experience full joy and happiness again.

The more I learned about my own illness, the more I realized that Jeff had been suffering in much the same way I had at his age. He showed all the symptoms, but I just didn't know what to look for. Initially I raged at a health care system that stigmatized and failed to address mental illnesses. I continued to be consumed with guilt that I somehow could have prevented Jeff's death.

Through therapy, I discovered that all those "what ifs" are a game we play with ourselves so we don't have to embrace the present reality. I have worked for a long time to learn how just to be present and to live knowing I did the best I could at the time. Over time, I've learned to feel grateful for the life I have, to see the amazing blessings I've received, and to know that I've been incredibly lucky despite experiencing such agony. Now that I am clean, sober, and successfully treating the depression that has plagued me for years, I am able to truly grasp reality and feel thankful for Jeff's life, though it was much shorter than any of us would have wished.

I've noticed that the better I feel, the calmer my wife and daughters feel. I keep a close eye on each of the kids and regularly do a pseudo-clinical checkup with them to indicate where they are in terms of depression or other moods. Thankfully, so far none of the girls have shown signs of depression.

Understanding what's going on inside the brain also helped me tremendously in dealing with my depression. Our brains are amazing, capable of making millions of calculations per second. Sometimes when I'm giving a presentation, I'll talk about how we are constantly making subconscious calculations and decisions based on those calculations, and I'll give an example from my football days. I'll throw a bottle of water to someone in the audience and talk about the arc, the velocity, the distance, and how they are able to instantly make all the calculations necessary to catch the pass.

We can train our brains to "think happy." We can reprogram negative thinking and behavior, and we can set up warning flags so we can take steps to recognize and cope with depression. People can increase their happiness by reframing things in a positive way, performing random acts of kindness, and counting their blessings.[10] Try it right now. Grab a pencil or pen, and hold it sideways in your teeth. This mimics smiling. Research has proven that when we smile, we actually change the brain's chemistry and neural pathways, opening up millions of additional connections and possibilities.

●　●　●

Actions to Avert Depression

1. SLEEP. Sleep is very important. Doctors at the University of Michigan Depression Center say that many men exhibiting signs of depression cannot reach the third and fourth realms of sleep, the deep stages where the actual cell restoration takes place, and recovery and energy building occur. Sometimes this is due to physical symptoms like sleep apnea, and sometimes it's due to depression or anxiety.

2. EXERCISE. Exercise also helps depression. Exercising may be the last thing you feel like doing when you're depressed, but push yourself a bit. Once your heart rate reaches a certain level, endorphins kick in, releasing a lot of happiness hormones throughout your system.

3. HAVE SEX. Enjoying an active, satisfying sexual relationship with a committed partner also staves off depression. According to Dr. Mehmet Oz, a frequent guest on *The Oprah Winfrey Show,* having sex regularly will add years to your life. Sex releases a cascade of feel-good chemicals throughout the entire body, improving the immune system and the brain's ability to process information.

4. CRY. Shedding tears helps relieve depression. Yes, I am talking about men crying. Shakespeare said, "Tears water our growth," and scientists have discovered that when we cry and really let loose with the waterworks, tears release a flow of healing hormones that affect every cell of the body. Crying boosts the immune system and releases endorphins and other hormones that promote feelings of well-being and connectedness.

After a good cry, you will actually feel better. I sometimes wonder whether the dramatic increase of heartburn and gastric reflux syndrome in men over the past 20 years is due to unshed tears. All those feelings men ignore and stuff away could end up eating them from inside out.

Crying isn't something that most guys want to do, let alone admit to, but inside even the toughest 300-pound professional linebackers, I have seen the most tender hearts and witnessed tears shed when those hearts are broken. For those who grieve, the tears honor the love we had for the person who has died. The tears remind us that we still are very much alive. Even though the heart we loved has stopped beating, our hearts don't have to stop loving.

5. USE LIGHT AND COLOR. Light and color can fight depression. Experts say spending just 10 minutes a day in unfiltered sunlight resets the body's hormonal system to its optimum, promoting healthy sleep and a general sense of well-being. Research has demonstrated that certain color combinations have been shown to elevate moods, while others tend to depress. I know that when I'm feeling depressed, everything seems either black or white, with few shades of gray and certainly few vibrant colors. I think this is why depressed people sometimes consider suicide.

If you feel you are limited to only two choices, black or white, neither may seem viable, and you may decide life just isn't worth living. I've learned that when I start feeling this way, spending time outdoors with the full spectrum of natural sunlight, all shades and tones of colors, can restore my soul. It seems to reset my internal chemistry, and it is one of the best ways to pull myself together when I'm feeling stressed. I remember escaping during college days, breaking away from the activity of a crowded campus into the adjoining canyon. I could just lie in a meadow for hours, gazing at the clouds passing overhead, listening to the wind blowing through the aspens, smelling the soil and the decaying leaves, and listening to the rushing water of the creek.

6. TRY MEDITATION, YOGA, MINDFULNESS, AND GRATITUDE. Several psychological studies have found that meditation, yoga, mindfulness, and gratitude make people happier. In a positive psychology class at George Mason University, the professor assigned each student four tasks: attending a yoga class, meditating for 15 minutes three days in a row, being mindful twice a day, and paying a gratitude visit to someone in his or her life. All these interventions increased the students' happiness, but the gratitude visits increased happiness the most.[11]

• • •

I have tried all of the above actions, and I have found the key for me is to recognize my depression triggers early, so I can take action. If you scored five or higher on the self-diagnostic depression checklist on page 54, or if you are experiencing any of the symptoms of depression mentioned in Chapter Six, you may very well benefit from a combination of treatments. It is certainly worthwhile to explore your options and see what works best for you. Because our brains are so complex, and because each of us carries a unique blueprint for optimal conditions, not one ideal therapy works equally well for all people. Be patient, and work with your doctor or therapist until you find the right combination of treatments to alleviate your symptoms. Just as no one factor triggers depression, no one "magic pill" will solve everyone's problems. Hang in there, and try not to get discouraged. Your patience will pay off when you finally find the best approach for you.

Chapter Nine

Calling New Plays

as one of my coaches used to say, "Life is 10 percent what happens to you and 90 percent how you respond to it." More than 500 research studies correlate optimism with improved health.[12] Studies have shown that happiness improves physical health and life span, and that positive emotions can even help people live 10 years longer.[13]

Sharing what I've learned helps me stay on top of my depression and helps heal my grief. It has given my life a renewed purpose and meaning that I never thought I'd have again. Scientists are announcing new discoveries daily that could improve so many people's lives dramatically. Yet, mental illnesses' stigma and society's perpetuation of the "tough guy" myth prevent many men from getting the help they so desperately need.

After participating in that initial panel at the University of Michigan Depression Center, the center asked if I might be willing to share my experiences with some groups. That launched something new in my life that has become tremendously important. I know that if I can get this information out to people, especially those who are suffering from depression and those who love someone who is depressed, I might be able to change their lives. I somehow feel that if I can save just one life, Jeff's death has not been not in vain. It comforts me to know that Jeff is doing as much in his death as he did in his life to help others.

Hopefully you and your loved ones can learn from my experience and perhaps gain some hope that will help you hang on and ultimately feel better. Since I started speaking to groups, I've traveled around the country presenting before sports organizations, fraternity houses, the Pentagon, college health clinics, leadership conferences, The Compassionate Friends organization (which helps families grieving the death of a child or sibling), and mental health professionals' conferences. I also have spoken on radio and TV to let depression sufferers know that there is a way out, and tomorrow can be better.

When I look back on my sports career, my family life, and my post-NFL business ventures, some patterns emerge that I have been able to see only in retrospect. I see how my behavior and choices along the way have led me to where I am now. Could I have been a better player? A better teammate? A better mentor? Sure. Could I have been a better son? A better husband? A better father? Of course! Could I have achieved great success in my businesses? Absolutely. But do any of these questions and answers change the past? Do they have any effect on the present or on the future? No.

I have learned that I need to embrace the life I have. I can see that so many people get caught up in regrets about the past. I've spent a lot of time in that mode, and it's terrifyingly easy to get lost in fears of the future: "How can I afford to put my kids through college?" "What if my spouse suffers from long-term health issues and we don't have insurance?" "How can I bear the pain of one more surgery on that troublesome sports injury?" "What if my child marries that boyfriend/girlfriend we all can't stand?"

Though they are grounded in reality, these questions bear a marked resemblance to those that kept me awake as a child: "What if the sun burns out and the earth becomes a cold marble of ice?" "What if a massive tidal wave strikes southern California and wipes out every house within 50 miles of the coast?" These mind games trap our energy in the future, rather than leaving it free so we can live fully in the present. I have realized that even if we map out intricate scenarios solving such dilemmas, the answers remain moot, because these problems have not (and may never) occur. You'll spend your energy far more effectively by focusing on the present. Do what you can to help others who are suffering, and just enjoy the gift of each additional breath that you are allowed to take in this life.

Life includes emotional and physical risks. If we drive, we can expect some dents. If we own a house, we can expect some emergency repairs. If we live, we can expect to get sick a few times. If we love, we can expect some broken hearts. Dr. Fred Luskin, who runs the Stanford Forgiveness Project, said, "A broken heart is part of love's equation."[14] Sometimes our hearts break because someone we loved has died. Sometimes it happens because a dream we've long cherished has died. Sometimes it happens because someone or something has harmed us, and we now feel we have no control over ourselves or what happens to us.

Recently, Dr. Luskin's and others' research has confirmed the value of forgiveness in the promotion of psychological, relationship, and physical health. "Forgiveness has been shown to reduce anger, hurt, depression, and stress, and lead to greater feelings of optimism, hope, compassion, and self-confidence."[15]

On September 14, 2006, Dr. Gloria Horsley and Dr. Heidi Horsley, the co-authors of this book, interviewed Columbine High

School massacre survivor Craig Scott on their radio show, *Healing the Grieving Heart.* Craig described the rage he felt after watching the gunmen murder his sister Rachel and 10 classmates. This fury was destroying him until a pastor told him, "Forgiveness is like setting a prisoner free and then finding out that prisoner is you." Today Craig and his father speak to audiences internationally about forgiveness and compassion.[16]

I have noticed that I sometimes start down the road to depression when I am angry or holding resentment against someone or something. Dr. Luskin suggests that once we forgive and release that resentment, we step onto the path to healing and happiness. The following is my take on his nine-step approach[17] to forgiving. Check it out, and you may find your own path to forgiveness.

●　●　●

My Thoughts about Dr. Luskin's Nine-Step Approach to Forgiveness

1. I have found it important to identify how I feel and then share it with others. (This book is a large part of this first step for me.)

2. I have committed to taking care of myself. I'm trying to eat right and take care of my body. I just had a much-needed knee surgery for an old football injury. I hope to resume exercising.

3. I try to take my life experiences less personally and change my grievance stories to ones of peace. I have found this step especially important because suicide creates a lot of blame and shame.

4. I try to live in the "now," focusing on the present and not on what hurt me two minutes — or 10 years — ago. A wise person put it this way: "The past is history, the future is a mystery, and the gift is now. That is why it is called *"the present."*

5. The moment I realize I am feeling upset, I practice simple stress management techniques to soothe my mind and relax my body. My favorite thing to do when I feel stressed is light a candle, sit down, and

focus on each breath I take as I look into the candle's flame.

6. I remind myself that I can hope for health, love, peace, and prosperity and that sometimes I don't need to work hard to get them. I simply need to allow them space in my life. I replay the positive messages coaches have given me over my years as a quarterback, as well as the love and encouragement my parents gave me as their son.

7. Instead of mentally replaying my hurts, I seek out new ways to make myself happy. I remember my quarterback training, during which we learned you can't look back; the last play is over and the next play is an opportunity.

8. I remember that a life well-lived is my best revenge. I try to notice the love, beauty, and kindness around me. I don't have to look far — I have a beautiful family, and I have learned to love myself again.

9. I slowly have learned to amend grievance stories and to forgive — I have found that when I forgive myself, I can forgive others more readily, and vice versa.

* * *

When I forgive, I reduce my anger, hurt, depression, and stress. I find hope, peace, compassion, and self-confidence. I recently met with a guy who said, "Okay, I've really screwed things up, and now I've just got to start over." I countered, "No, you don't want to start over. You want to remember all those things you did wrong and forgive yourself. Do not regret your mistakes, but learn from them." I told him it's like burning your hand on the stove. You don't want to forget that, because you don't want to put your hand on the stove again; it becomes a learning experience. You actually can feel thankful for that first burn, because it taught you to stay away from the heat, averting more serious burns. I asked this guy to stop the next time he feels he can't go on anymore, and think beyond the regrets to all the positives in his life.

If you feel you can no longer go on, think about any good aspects of your life. I have made a short list of possibilities that I frequently think about.

• • •

Can You Feel Grateful
for Any of the Following?

- At least one person in the world loves me.

- Life is a gift.

- I've got $10, $1, or one dime in my pocket; that's better than nothing.

- I have my health.

- I still can take a breath.

- I can see the sky, wonder about the wind, sing a song, have a taste of chocolate, or play with my dog.

• • •

I asked my young friend not to think of it as starting over but instead as forming a new game plan. I asked him to remember his most important asset in achieving that game plan: hope.

Obviously, support from others helps a lot. Most of us have a circle of people who love us. When we are depressed or in despair, however, we may perceive the situation incorrectly, thinking, "Well, this person doesn't love me because he yelled at me," or, "That person is mad at me — I've let her down." Remember that these perceptions aren't necessarily true. These people are trying to help, but your depression may make you perceive them in a negative way. I've found it important to own up, accept the things I've done in the past, and forgive myself...because other people will forgive me. And if they don't forgive me right away because they no longer trust me, in the long run, I don't care how long it takes. I know I will be able to build some trust in a relationship again. But I can't erase everything and start over, because I'll probably repeat the same mistakes. So when I hear someone say, "I'm going to start over," I say, "No. I don't want you to start over. I want you to forgive yourself and remember your past actions. Remember that they did have consequences that you do not want to repeat. Now you can formulate a game plan."

Your game plan should include those who helped you, who stood on the sidelines offering support and encouragement when you were down. Once you finally can acknowledge that they *do* love you and that you can love yourself, you can sit down and figure out how to move forward. You can start thinking positively again, with a sense of purpose in life. I've heard folks use the phrase, "Cultivate an attitude of gratitude." Doing so has helped me realize one of my purposes in life: to help lift others.

In accordance with Dr. Luskin's and Dr. Neimeyer's belief that hope, connection, and meaning create a satisfying life, Dr. Gloria and Dr. Heidi have recently created The Open to Hope Foundation. This foundation provides resources, support, and guidance to those suffering a loss. Dr. Luskin, Dr. Neimeyer, and I serve on the board, and we are committed to promoting hope throughout the world. Dr. Gloria, Dr. Heidi, Dr. Luskin, Dr. Neimeyer, and I have something else in common: each has survived the death of an immediate family member. We have all traveled that painful journey through grief and found forgiveness, meaning, and hope along the way. We know we can spend our time obsessing over the events surrounding these deaths, or we can pay tribute to loved ones we have lost and celebrate their lives. We prefer to spend our energy spreading hope and healing, trying to leave the world better than we found it.

Young or old, human beings are faced with certain risk factors that can act as triggers to depression. Whether from this book, my speaking engagements, or informal discussions, I hope that those who are hurting realize: *You are not alone. Help is out there. You can feel better again.* If you can be brutally honest with yourself and admit that you are not feeling like you should, then you can take the next step and seek help. You owe it to yourself to get help. You are here for a reason, and you deserve to love the life you live.

I ask you to turn to page 54, to the Nine-Symptom Checklist for Depression. If you think you are depressed or want to learn the symptoms of depression, take the test now or give it to a friend or family member. If this doesn't apply to you right now, go ahead and skip the checklist. Keep reading, but remember that the first step toward treating depression is recognizing the symptoms. Depression is treatable, like any other disease. If you take the test and score in the depression range, don't keep it to yourself. Share your results with your family, friends, and definitely with a doctor (consider taking this book to your doctor). Take action!

Working with the
University of Michigan Depression Center

I never want to see anyone experience the pain my son suffered or the aftermath our family endured. This is why I am passionate about learning as much as I can about depression and suicide, and about educating anyone who will listen. One of the most rewarding aspects of my life has been my association with the University of Michigan Center for Depression. Since I first became acquainted with the organization and its goals, I've given hundreds of speeches and presentations to athletic organizations, professional conferences, and mental health institutes around the country, and I've felt honored to provide one-on-one insight for some very special people. I've learned and grown by listening to so many other men experiencing depression or dealing with suicide.

●　●　●

Obviously, each situation is unique, and each person has many options available. I think all the people I've had the privilege of meeting needed to know hope still existed. Spreading the word that help is available, that hope is possible, has given meaning to the profound loss of my son Jeff. I hope that you will share this information with someone who needs it, and I hope that each person this book reaches will know that he is not alone.

Thank you for reading this book. I am closing with "Nine Things Everyone Should Know about Mental Illness," because so many people out there are suffering. Though they are calling their best plays, may they know that education and coaching can greatly increase their odds of winning. I would advise them: Don't try to do it alone; remember that without a team, there is no game.

— Best wishes, Eric Hipple

● ● ●

Nine Things Everyone Should Know About Mental Illness

1. The human brain regulates all forms of behavior.
2. Mental illnesses are disorders of the brain that disrupt thoughts, behaviors, moods, and relationships.
3. Mental illnesses are not weaknesses, nor are they character defects.
4. The causes of mental illnesses can be physical, psychological, or a combination of both.
5. Mental illnesses are treatable.
6. The majority of the severely mentally ill are not receiving appropriate treatment.
7. Severe mental illness affects one in every five families in this country.
8. Roughly 37 percent of alcohol abusers and 53 percent of drug abusers also have at least one serious mental illness.
9. Ignorance about mental illnesses leads to stigma and unfair treatment.

The above is adapted from a list compiled by the Mental Illness Research Association

Epilogue

throughout my life, a number of people have supported me through some terrible experiences. At times I thought people didn't care, and I often didn't care what people thought. I was the quarterback, in charge and calling the plays. I felt free to do my own thing, and I thought that was the way it should be. It took Jeff's suicide and some very self-destructive behavior to change my attitude.

Ernie Romer, whom I met in 1992, has been one of my greatest supporters. He kept track of me throughout my bankruptcy and Jeff's suicide. One day, about five years after Jeff's death, Ernie called me and said, "When you're ready, I'm here to help you get back into business." I had dropped my insurance license and was going after what I felt was my calling and mission: speaking about depression and suicide prevention. I told Ernie about this, and he advised me to take my time and go ahead and fulfill my mission. I owe him a lot, as he gave me the encouragement I needed to go on.

Today I am happy to say that I have found a balance in my life between working as the outreach representative for the University of Michigan Depression Center and selling insurance. I work with individuals who need help and support. I don't give advice, because I believe people already know what they need but are putting up walls. They're putting up illusions and fake fronts and justifying their behavior; they're not really owning up to their mistakes.

This reminds me of the quarterback who throws a bad pass and says, "Well, the guy ran the wrong route." Or a receiver who misses a ball and says, "Oh, the lights were in my eyes." Yeah, those things happen, but ultimately the ball hit you in the hands, and you should have caught it. So, let's get rid of the excuses and just own up to our actions. Only then can we improve.

When I talk with people, I tell them that life moves forward. The game goes on. You could throw in the towel, take off your helmet, walk off the field, and retreat to the locker room. Guess what? Nobody's going to give a damn, because the game goes on. But that's not what we want. We want to participate in the game and participate in life. We want to attain our goals, contribute to the team, and score touchdowns. We want to fulfill the purpose in our life. The ultimate goal is to have a winning attitude and to accept life as it comes.

The University of Michigan Depression Center is doing phenomenal work and hopes to become part of a national network of depression centers. The Center has allowed me to go out to high schools and speak to the kids. This is a real thrill for me, because I know some of them are going through difficulties. I know some of them are having problems they don't want to talk about because they're afraid of what other people will think. It is amazing to be able to talk to kids and give them the idea that they can talk to others. They can share their stories and find that others have the same thoughts. Kids can be really high-risk and hard to reach, but once you connect with them, they're often more vocal than adults. They're very honest. They bring up points that may not even occur to adults. All we can do is coach them the best we can, and help them remember that they can regain lost trust. They can have lives. They can survive this!

Thankfully, my girls are flourishing, and my wife Shelly is doing wonderfully well. She's working for the University of Michigan Dermatology Department, and she loves her job. She's probably the happiest I've ever seen her. I think that's partly because I'm living a life of which she can be proud. And it shows. It's great. Also, we've been able to put a lot of the pain of Jeff's suicide behind us. Although we'll never forget Jeff or how he died, we're able to move on with love and understanding.

At the time this book was finished, my oldest daughter Erica was 26 and working at a law firm in Washington, D.C. Erica was a senior in high school when Jeff shot himself. They went through a lot together during the divorce and were very close. Despite this horrific tragedy, she went on to graduate and attended the University of Utah, where she received her bachelor's degree in political science. She is a resilient, intelligent, amazing woman and a wonderful role model for her two younger sisters. I am very proud of her. As Erica reminded me, even though our family has experienced extreme highs and lows, we've come a long way and always have stuck together. We continue to be a work in progress.

Taylor was a 17-year-old senior when this book was finished. She danced at the Fenton Dance Academy and was on the yearbook staff at Hartland High School. She has a great command of the English language, including an amazing vocabulary. Taylor is a talented writer and does great comic impersonations, just like her big brother did. She's a good student and gets along well with her peers. She suffers from Obsessive Compulsive Disorder, which was a little scary for a while, but she has come to grips with it. She sees a counselor, and I think she now feels comfortable in her own skin.

Our little Tarah was 15, a sophomore, and a poet. She is outgoing and loves kids. Tarah will talk to anyone and wears her heart on her sleeve. She went through quite a traumatic time because she was in the house when Jeff shot himself, and it had a profound effect on her. However, Tarah has been able to express herself through poetry. In fact, two of her poems have been published so she's been able to reach out that way. I was so proud of her when she decided to get up and talk in front of her class about depression and the risks of suicide. I was very impressed that a high school sophomore could speak about her brother's death. I was even more impressed that the teacher asked her to stay and talk to the third-period and fourth-period classes. It was so neat to get a phone call from her and hear her say, "Dad, guess what I did? I talked to people about Jeff's suicide and how they can help each other." The following is one of Tarah's poems.

THE POLISHED STONE
By Tarah Hipple

Dedicated to my brother, Jeff

I looked at the picture,
And it made me break down in tears,
With my hand over my mouth,
I then close the door so nobody hears.
It explains everything,
With your name polished on the rock,
To the polished basketball shoes,
And the last door that you ever locked.
I guess you didn't know what to do,
And I guess you never knew what to say,
I guess you couldn't put it into words,
But it all came to the conclusion of your last day.

I cross my heart,

And I'll hope to die,

I swear I'll believe you,

But, please, tell me that hopeful lie.

That you will come back,

And you will stay my brother,

That you will never leave us,

And you will stay forever.

This picture was a memory that I never had,

I have never seen your polished stone,

I can never express how much I miss you,

And how I feel so alone.

I just want you to know,

That you are in my dreams every night,

You are in my dreams of, what used to be, a complete family,

But now, I am sometimes in the darkness,

Yet I am happy you are always in the light.

Your basketball shoes,

Secretly had wings on the side,

I'll never forget that this was your dream,

But, Jeff, I just can't say goodbye.

Our family is finally in a place where we can honor, celebrate, and pay tribute to Jeff's life instead of focusing solely on his death. It has been a long journey, but we finally have found hope, joy, and peace again. Although we are poorer for having lost Jeff, we are so much richer for having known him for 15 years. He will remain forever in our hearts.

Special Words for Coaches
and Others Who Work with Children

recently participated in the Nike Coach of the Year Clinic held in Pennsylvania. The director of the program was former high school coach Jim Tkach. The presentations, discussions, and comments led me to include some advice particularly for coaches, teachers, and those who work with children.

Positive Framework. Remember that those who are grieving, suffering from depression, or struggling with a hard time in their lives sometimes don't respond well to the traditional coach communication style (which unfortunately includes screaming, yelling, and similar "command and control" stuff). We've gotten better results by approaching the situation from a positive framework. We've realized that as coaches, we sometimes fill parental roles; the kids will come to us because they respect us.

Watch for Stressors. As a coach or teacher, remember: you have the ability to ruin or really improve a life, just as a counselor or gatekeeper exerts influence. People experience stresses throughout life, and kids do get down. Stressors can include moving, losing a family member, the divorce of parents, conflicts with friends, relationship problems, or health issues. Participating in sports also can create stress for a kid. Maybe he gets hurt. Maybe she's not a starter. Maybe he's not fulfilling his dream. Maybe her father is screaming at her or making her feel that she's not living up to his expectations. Maybe his coach doesn't like his personality.

The Making of a Good Coach. Over the course of my life, I have figured out what makes a good coach. In my mind, Jim Tkach, whose son also committed suicide, is an excellent coach. Detroit Lions Coach Rod Marinelli, who was an assistant coach to my Utah State team, is an excellent coach. Terry Shea, who served as my quarterback coach at Utah State is an excellent coach. These guys get it. The common ingredient among these coaches is their positive leadership style; they get the players to *want* to win, rather than beating them over the head with fear. Take some of the stress off, and they'll play better. Make it so they don't have to think on the field, so they think at practice. It's hard to think at practice when someone's screaming at you. Make them think on their assignments, so they just react when they get on the field. They should react and play well *because they want to,* because they love the game, and because they love the person leading them.

Let Everyone Share in the Glory. Personal pride makes for winning teams and enthusiastic players. But as a coach, whom do you really want to recognize? Yes, the guy who goes for a touchdown. The guy who is your top, star player. Of course you've got to recognize him. But some guys on your team are never going to play, yet they show up day in and day out for practice. They're the practice team, the guys who won't get into the game unless you're ahead by 40. The best time to talk to the people not playing is when one of your top players scores a touchdown. Walk over, sit down next to the guys who aren't playing, and say, "Do you know why that guy scored?

Do you know why that guy is good? It's because of you. Because of the effort you put in every day at practice. Without you, he would not be able to do that. Your hard work is what drives him, what makes his job possible – because *you're* giving him a good look." That's how you solidify a team, because now everybody is sharing the glory.

Keep Everyone Involved. As a coach, you've got to let the team know that you're watching and evaluating everybody — not negatively, but positively. So, if you look over and you see kids sitting on their helmets, kind of looking the other way and not paying attention, you've got to let them know. Maybe at the end of practice, sit down and reiterate to the whole team that you are keeping a close eye on everyone, and they will not get a chance to play unless they act like part of the team. To be part of the team, they must be involved.

Tell them, "You must encourage the person next to you. When somebody does something well, I want to hear from the rest of you." This helps avoid that lower-class/higher-class mentality in which suddenly all the good guys are playing and the guys who aren't playing are on the dummy squad or the second or third team. Suddenly no one is using them. They're sitting on their helmets. They're not paying attention, and the coach isn't paying attention to them. He's never encouraging them, and they have no hope of ever getting in the game. The more the coach sees them sitting on their helmets and not paying attention, the less likely he is to put them in the game, because he thinks he can't depend on them.

It's All About Teamwork. As a coach, you have to let the players know up front that each of them is extremely important to the team, that you love each and every one of them. Make them the best people they can be, and let them know this is a team concept. If you do this, you solidify a team. You bring them together as one, and they respect you for that. They also start respecting each other. The star player realizes that the guy who doesn't get to play is cheering for him. The guy who doesn't get to play is working really hard in practice to give the star player a better look. That kind of teamwork is very important.

Build Self-Esteem. Not every player on your team has had the same luck in upbringing, genetics, and breaks that others have had — but every one of them still deserves the dignity of being treated as a human being and as a potential positive for humanity. They can do something. Maybe you think a guy's never going to play, but he might if you give him the right positive feedback and encouragement. This guy might become a doctor. He may succeed in yet another field. You just don't know. But you can't cut kids like this off at the heels. You can't degrade them or push them off and lower their self-esteem. If they're already feeling down because of depressive issues, negative thoughts, or problems at home, they'll rarely have a chance to get up. They won't gain the self-esteem to accomplish what they could with good leadership. A good coach builds self-esteem on and off the field.

Life Coaching: Working with Families

In the course of my presentations, concerned family members often ask for my perspective. Following are situations that I have seen repeatedly. I hope they will help to address some of your concerns. To protect the confidentiality of my discussions, I have changed the names and details. Although I am not a professional counselor, I always give a listening ear. Like the coaches who have impacted my life, I try to provide encouragement and hope. I think of myself as more of a life coach, drawing from my personal experience and the experiences of others who have crossed my path. Here are some family situations I see frequently and my take on them.

●　●　●

Situation: *A high school teacher and parent of three teenagers asks me how to recognize signs of depression in teens.*

My Take on It: As a player, coach, and parent, I think it is difficult to recognize depression in kids. They are changing so fast, going through so many ups and downs, but I tell parents and teachers to look for dramatic changes in behavior: a child who is outgoing suddenly becomes withdrawn; a teenager without a religious background surprisingly turns very religious; a formerly calm child becomes extremely irritable; a teen begins acting out, for example fighting or bullying; a teen begins giving away prized possessions; or a formerly diligent student has a dramatic drop in school grades. I also tell families and teachers to be aware of life events that precipitate depression: death of a family member or friend; parents divorcing; moving far away; and other sudden life changes and dislocations.

* * *

Situation: *A distraught mother and father ask me how to get help for their reluctant son who has been exhibiting signs of depression.*

My Take on It: It can be difficult to convince someone who doesn't feel like living that help is available and that he will feel better if he seeks it. As the old saying goes, "You can bring a horse to water, but you can't make it drink."

When we are down, we need to trust that we will find hope again for a winning game or season. Imagine you have never heard of the flu, but now you have it. You wake up every morning for three or four days in a row, throwing up, aching, and feeling feverish and completely miserable. How long do you think you can go on like that before you lose the will to live? Well, if somebody tells you that you are suffering from an illness called the flu, which typically lasts about two weeks, you feel less hopeless. You might think, "Oh, okay. In that case, I can hang on, because I know things will change eventually."

We can help somebody to understand that help is available, that his life contains limitless possibilities if he'll just hang on, and that he doesn't have to live with the pain endlessly. Hold on to hope. As Winston Churchill said, "...never give in, never give in, never, never, never, never..." Sometimes when people are deeply depressed, as this young man was, they can't see hope. We have to share our hope with them and let them know that we're there and that we are going to help them through it for as long as it takes.

● ● ●

Situation: *A young wife tells me her husband is sending out all the signals that he is in distress and deeply depressed. She wonders how to provide* real *help — not just a pat on the head and assurance that life will get better.*

My Take on It: I advised this young wife she must get her husband properly diagnosed and into treatment. Her husband needs to know about the available treatment possibilities, and he needs to hear that he doesn't have to live with the intense pain and depression. With therapy and medication, he can and will feel better.

● ● ●

Situation: *A mom and dad whose son killed himself are now filled with regret and feelings of inadequacy, and they are wondering how they can parent their two remaining children.*

My Take on It: As the parent of three daughters and a son who took his own life, I really identify with these parents. After Jeff killed himself, I kept searching for answers. I often felt like my mind was on fast-forward, but I kept pushing the replay button. "What did I do wrong as a dad?" "How could it have been different?" "Why did he do it?" The stigma made it hard to talk with others. If you tell someone that a loved one died in a car crash, the listener immediately expresses sympathy — after all, a terrible thing happened to an innocent person. If you tell them that your child died by suicide, they don't know how to respond.

Of course, I felt tremendous guilt and regret. I felt responsible. I should have seen it coming and stopped it. I became very self-destructive for a period of time following my son's suicide. I thought about my own father — I can't imagine anyone being a better dad. He never missed my games, and he was always there for me. Even so, he never noticed I was depressed as a young man. He was not a perfect man, not that any are, but everything he did was heartfelt and filled with love. Losing the chance to finish parenting Jeff is one of the most painful aspects of his death, because I always wanted to be the kind of father to Jeff that my dad was to me. Although I can't have that father-son relationship, I do have three daughters whom I love very much.

I advised these parents that, even in their grief, it's important to put themselves into the shoes of their other children, to realize that these children are also grieving, missing their sibling. They now require even more empathic parenting than ever before, and they need help getting through this tough time. Like quarterbacks, mothers and fathers make decisions based on the information and resources on hand at the time. Like athletes, parents regret past performances, whether a child has died or not. Balancing regrets is key to staying in the game, and we must remember that we did the best we could at the time. We are trying our best now, and regrets only keep our energy in the past, rather than allowing us to focus on the present.

"What could have beens" will undo us if we let them. I told these parents that, like quarterbacks, we each possess a general "playbook." We formulate our decisions based on previous plans, but sometimes we also need to make fast choices based on the situation at hand.

Throughout my professional career I had experienced many changes in coaches (over the course of 10 years, I had three different head coaches and five offensive coordinators). Although I would have liked to have had the same coach my entire career, the differences between each coach made me a stronger, more strategic player. I suggested to this couple that they expand the network of adults available to their children, that they consider adding other teammates who could bring some normalcy to a very stressful situation. I also suggested that these parents not be afraid to ask others for help — as bereaved parents, we have gone through one of the hardest human experiences, so we need to treat each other and ourselves with compassion.

● ● ●

Situation: *A young man wonders how to help a buddy suffering business and marriage failures.*

My Take on It: I told this young man about my good friend and business associate, Jordan Raider, who had provided invaluable support after Jeff's death. Jordan stood by me through both my DUI and my business troubles. I thought I knew Jordan well, but I didn't know that when Jordan was young, his father had committed suicide. He told me that there was a lot of stigma attached to suicide when he was a child, and he wasn't encouraged to talk about how he was feeling. Jordan's experience made him want to help ease my pain and just listen. With Jordan I can be myself, experience what I'm feeling, and know that he won't judge me. He'll just be there with me.

I suggested to this young man that he try to just be there for his buddy, that he didn't have to offer earth-shattering counsel. Just let him be himself, voice his concerns, and, most importantly, let him know that he is not alone. I gave him the signs of depression and possible suicide risk, which appear on page 56 of this book, and told him to get help if his friend exhibited any of the signs. People don't always understand that, most often, the person doesn't want to die — but at that moment, he or she sees no other way out, no other solution. If you can get the suicidal person through a 24-hour period, you can usually prevent that suicide.

• • •

Situation: *A former soldier who had just completed his tour of duty in Afghanistan feels deeply discouraged because he lost many close friends in the war. Since returning home, he has been suffering survivor's guilt and wonders whether he can go on.*

My Take on It: When I met with this young man, we initially just sat together and said nothing, just let the feelings settle in. When he felt ready to talk, I listened to his story about the friends he had lost and what he'd seen in Afghanistan. It took quite a while for him to tell me about all the unimaginable horrors he'd experienced there. When he was finished, I said, "To be honest with you, I don't know if I could live with that, either. But I do know what it's like to be on the other end when somebody takes his life. I know what that feels like."

Then I said, "Based on what you told me, man, I can understand why you would want to take your life. But I also have to tell you what's going to happen if you do it. The pain you feel right now is going to impact about 20 other people: your mother, family, the people who love you, other friends, people who know you. It's going to ripple through to people you don't even know but who know what you've gone through, and it's going to hurt them." I explained how those he left behind would be feeling the same pain he was experiencing now. He not only would be ending his life, but he also would be hurting others. I asked him whether he really wanted to put that on somebody else and suggested he think about it before making any decisions. We left it at that. About a month and a half later, he called me, said he was doing better, and thanked me for giving him a dose of reality. Perhaps since I've seen both sides of the fence, suicide is not an option for me anymore, and now it's probably not an option for him, either.

• • •

Situation: *A 35-year-old man is critically depressed but doesn't want to go to the hospital for treatment. He wonders whether he should end his life because he is suffering so much.*

My Take on It: I first asked him, "Why do you want to die?" I told him that if he really wanted to stop hurting, he could achieve that in other ways.

If he wanted to die for another reason, we could talk about it and explore the issues. I looked at him for a moment, and I thought about the great coaches who had taught me and how they would ask me to analyze a situation. I said to this young guy, "Let's see. You are here, so some part of you must want to live. If not, you'd probably have killed yourself already. Let's explore that aspect for a moment."

He then started thinking about his choices and the extreme ending he was considering. Our discussion brought him into a reflective mode, in which we discussed the pain he was experiencing and the reasons he was feeling as he did. Even more importantly, the discussion offered an option out — a way to solve his problem other than ending his life. Sometimes just acknowledging the profound pain someone is feeling is the first step to healing, and it opens the door to options to move beyond the pain.

• • •

Situation: *A man recently committed suicide, devastating his entire family. The man's wife lost her husband and doesn't know how to talk to their two young children about it. The man's parents lost their only son. The man's teenage sister lost her beloved older brother. The* *family members wonder how they will ever come together.*

My Take on It: As I spoke with this heartsick family, I realized that all of them were grieving in different ways. The wife was dealing not only with her husband's suicide, but also with her new role as both mother and father. She felt heavily burdened with all her husband's former tasks, with diminished resources.

The parents, who were also grandparents, were so intensely grieving their boy's death they had almost forgotten that their teenage daughter had lost her brother. The man's father felt angry because a handbook had suggested that he could have prevented the suicide had he been a better father. The man's mother felt sad and had withdrawn into silence, leaving all the outward emotions to her enraged husband. The man's teenage sister deeply missed the brother she had idolized.

Through the lens of my NFL training, I immediately saw that to survive this experience together, the family members needed to start working as one and get on the same page of the playbook. I told them that, as with football, there are many different responses to the game of life, and they don't have to grieve in the same way. They simply need to respect the different styles of grieving, the different timelines, and each other's right to grieve. This will help them bridge their differences, as it did for my family after Jeff's suicide.

I also recommended they attend a grief support group, which also includes separate groups for each type of loss — spouse, child, and sibling. I thought that in a small group the man's young wife would have a chance to share her experience and learn from others in similar situations, especially how to discuss the death with her children. The man's father then became the team leader. He said he could see that if my family could make it, his could, too. I agreed with him and said I believed that by getting through a traumatically painful period together, they could become a stronger family. They eventually would get to the other side, where they could honor their dead loved one in peace.

● ● ●

Situation: *A middle-aged man loses his job after more than 25 years with his company. Now he feels like a failure because he can no longer provide for his family.*

My Take on It: I've noticed that, unfortunately, many of us equate our value with our paycheck. Even when we choose to give up that paycheck, such as through retirement, we can become depressed if we cannot support our families as we did before. We feel even worse when we have no choice in the decision, such as when business closures, layoffs, or health issues force us to stop working. The auto industry's decline has caused an especially large problem in the Detroit area, where I live.

The man told me he hadn't had any success looking for another job, and he increasingly felt that his family would be better off if he were dead and they collected his life insurance. I asked him whether the only value he contributed to the family was financial support. He revealed that he was close to his children, and that other than the money problems, he and his wife had a strong marriage.

He disclosed that he was especially upset that his daughter's marriage was approaching because he could no longer afford to give her the wedding of her dreams. I asked him if he thought his daughter really equated his love with how much he planned to spend on her wedding, and whether he thought she would rather walk down the aisle without him. Would she rather have a grand fairytale ceremony without him or have him at her side and scale back her plans? He admitted that he had figured out he could budget enough money for a nice wedding, and his daughter would prefer his presence.

We talked a lot longer, and he said his wife and daughters valued him for the love and leadership he provided, and how they felt about him did not depend on his livelihood. With this awareness, he became willing to discuss some options for handling the pain he was feeling. The man agreed to go to therapy and to discuss antidepressant options with his doctor. He contacted me several months later and said that the medication immediately alleviated the pain and distress, and the therapy helped him see more options available to him. He also reported that the wedding took place at their home, that his daughter was a lovely bride, and that he was in the interview process with several prospective new jobs.

Acknowledgments

I want to thank Pat and Wayne Loder of The Compassionate Friends for asking me to be the Marshall for the TCF Walk to Remember at the National Conference in Dearborn, Michigan, in July 2006. It was there that I met Drs. Gloria and Heidi Horsley and subsequently was asked to serve as a board member for their Open to Hope Foundation and to be a guest on their inspirational radio show, *Open to Hope.* As a result of hearing my story and making a heartfelt connection between the death of Gloria's son Scott (Heidi's brother) and my son Jeff, the three of us began an extraordinary journey of turning my life story into a book.

I thank my wonderful wife Shelly and our two daughters, Taylor and Tarah, for my life, heart, and soul; and my oldest daughter Erica, who continues to give me inspiration and love. I thank my father and mother for cheering me on during good times, and for seeing me through the bad. I appreciate the sacrifices made to support me during my years of football. Thanks to my siblings, Mike, Liz, and Missy, who have continued to be at my side and love me unconditionally. Thanks to my in-laws, the Rhoades family, for accepting me for who I am, and to my ex-wife Jann Parker, Jeff's mother, for giving Jeff life.

I thank all of my coaches over the years and those who support high school, college, and professional teams. I especially want to thank the Detroit Lions for providing me with a career and the chance of a lifetime, and to the fans for cheering me on through 10 years of victory and defeat. Go for it, Detroit Lions! Go, Junior!

My sincere heartfelt thanks to my neighbors Tom and Heidi Roberts, who were at our side early on and helped my family through the unimaginable; to my friends at Lake Shannon for their unending support; to Tibor and Tom Gyarmati, for being there for me during those early hours and for their continued friendship and understanding; to Karen Marshall for sitting with me in my grief, mentoring me, and sharing her soul; and to Tim Pendell for always being a part of my journey.

I thank my publisher Karla Wheeler, Kelly Brachle, and the entire team at Quality of Life Publishing Co. for believing in my story and for working diligently to coordinate countless details. Thanks also to editor Beverly McManus and to Karen Lau for her tireless transcription. All of you have made this the book that it is.

Most of all, I want to thank my son Jeff. Even though he was only in my life for 15 short years, he taught me about compassion, forgiveness, and the depth of a father's love.

Afterword

We first met Eric in Dearborn, Michigan, during The Compassionate Friends National Conference. Eric served as the honorary leader of the Sunday Walk to Remember, and his presence was dynamic. He seemed a natural-born leader as thousands of people followed him through the streets of Dearborn, walking in remembrance of their deceased children and siblings.

We are a mother-daughter team hosting *Open to Hope,* an Internet radio show for those who grieve, and we serve on the national board level with The Compassionate Friends. Eric was coordinating a butterfly release at the Walk when we asked him to be a guest on our show. He flashed his big, teddy bear smile and replied, "Sure." We later learned that Eric is constantly on the road speaking about suicide prevention, grief, and depression. He tirelessly helps others heal after their losses.

With Eric's input, we called the show "Real Men Do Cry." During our radio broadcast, Eric impressed us with his honesty, sincerity, and openness regarding his lifelong struggle with depression and the suicide of his 15-year-old son, Jeff. Because an auto accident had killed our beloved son/brother, Scott, at age 17, we shared some similar feelings of loss and tragedy. Eric had amazing advice and wisdom, as well as a keen understanding of men's struggles with depression and their challenges. A tough former athlete with real-life experience, he was willing to bare his soul and show his vulnerability to the world.

Many men could identify with Eric; he had suffered numerous emotions, including anger, rage, disgust, sadness, and despair, and gone on to create change. The veteran NFL quarterback proceeded to help others after his only son died of suicide. He has spread the word that depression is a disease and that, with help, people can survive severe loss and find hope again. Eric's keen sense of humor and perspective on his life can be seen in one of this book's chapter titles: "Monday Night Football to Monday Night in Jail."

We often have noted that females comprise three-quarters or more of support groups and grief conferences, and we therefore feel that Eric brings a greatly needed male voice to the world of grief and loss. He is not the voice of a therapist or counselor, but that of a regular guy with personal experience and important information to share. Eric continues to inspire us with all he has accomplished in the hopes of saving at least one life as a tribute to Jeff. He was an unforgettable guest.

Several months after the show aired, we contacted Eric and asked him if he would endorse our new book, *Teen Grief Relief: Parenting With Understanding, Support and Guidance,* (Rainbow Books, Inc., 2007). He most graciously agreed. Eric then said, "Hey, I've been wanting to write a book about my life and work. Why don't you write it with me?" How could we refuse this enthusiastic, spirited, driven man? How could we turn down the opportunity of a lifetime of helping Eric deliver his message? We were honored to help Eric deliver the message that Jeff's life counted, and that, even in death, he was helping others and saving lives. How wonderful to have a real guy open his heart and bare his soul to reach out to those in pain.

Eric's enthusiasm is infectious, and so we began a yearlong journey. We interviewed Eric, his coaches, family, friends, and former football players. Some highlights of our journey include visiting the Detroit Lions Training Camp and discovering what it's like to be an NFL quarterback, as well as visiting the University of Michigan Depression Center and learning about its state-of-the-art depression treatments.

We always find writing a book difficult as well as fun. Will we ever get it done? Can we make the first touchdown? Well, here is the book in its entirety, and we think it's a winner! We hope Eric's life, his work, and his courage will be an inspiration in your life as it has been in ours.

— Gloria C. Horsley, Ph.D.,
and Heidi Horsley, Psy.D.

Notes

Chapter 5: Tackled by Life

1   *Detroit Free Press* (November 8, 1989).

Chapter 6: Monday Morning Quarterbacking

2   San Francisco Suicide Prevention Hotline; Website: www.sfsuicide.org

3   National Institute of Mental Health; Website: www.menanddepression.nimh.nih.gov/health/publications/men-and-depression/suicide.shtml

4   Ibid.

5   Horsley H, Patterson T; *The Effects of a Parent Guidance Intervention on Communication among Adolescents who have Experienced the Sudden Death of a Sibling* (The Journal of American Family Therapy) 34: 119-137.

6   Packman W, Horsley H, Davies B, Kramer R; *Continuing Bonds Following the Death of a Sibling* (Death Studies Journal; 2007) 30: 817-841.

7   Neimeyer R; *Meaning Reconstruction and the Experience of Loss* (American Psychological Association; 2001).

8   National Institute of Mental Health; Website: www.menanddepression.nimh.nih.gov/health/publications/suicide-in-the-us-statistics-and-prevention.shtml

9   San Francisco Suicide Prevention Hotline; Website: www.sfsuicide.org

Chapter 8: Making a Comeback

10   Stambor Z; *Is Our Happiness Set in Stone?* (Monitor on Psychology; December 2007).

11   Max DT; (The New York Times Magazine; 2007).

Chapter 9: Calling New Plays

12   Lambert C; *The Science of Happiness: Psychology Explores Humans at their Best* (Harvard Magazine; 2007).

13   Max DT; (The New York Times Magazine; 2007).

14   Luskin F; *Forgive for Good: A Proven Prescription for Health and Happiness* (HarperCollins; New York; 2002). www.learningtoforgive.com/about.htm

15   The Stanford Forgiveness Project. Website: www.learningtoforgive.com/about.htm

16   www.thegriefblog.com

17   Luskin F; *Forgive for Good: A Proven Prescription for Health and Happiness* (HarperCollins; New York; 2002). www.learningtoforgive.com/about.htm

Resources

American Foundation for Suicide Prevention (AFSP) — AFSP is a national not-for-profit organization exclusively dedicated to understanding and preventing suicide through research, education, and advocacy, and to reaching out to people with mental disorders and those impacted by suicide. (www.afsp.org) 1-888-333-AFSP (2377)

The Compassionate Friends (TCF) — TCF assists families toward the positive resolution of grief following the death of a child of any age and provides information to help others be supportive. (www.compassionatefriends.org) 1-877-969-0010

Open to Hope — *Open to Hope* is an Internet radio show dedicated to those who have lost loved ones. Shows are archived on www.opentohope.com. Books published by the Open to Hope Foundation include: *Open to Hope: Inspirational Stories of Healing After Loss;* and *Open to Hope: Inspirational Stories for Handling the Holidays After Loss.*

Horsley H, Horsley G; *Teen Grief Relief: Parenting with Understanding, Support, and Guidance* (Rainbow Books, Inc.; Florida; 2007).

Horsley H, Patterson T; *The Effects of a Parent Guidance Interven-*

tion on Communication among Adolescents who have Experienced the Sudden Death of a Sibling (The Journal of American Family Therapy; 2006) 34:119-137.

Lambert C; *The Science of Happiness: Psychology Explores Humans at their Best* (Harvard Magazine; 2007).

National Suicide Hotline — Your call will be routed to the service center closest to you; 24-hour, toll free. 1-800-SUICIDE (784-2433)

National Suicide Prevention Lifeline — 24-hour, toll-free. (www.suicidepreventionlifeline.org) 1-800-273-TALK (8255)

National Institute of Mental Health — (www.menanddepression.nimh.nih.gov/index.shtml)

Neimeyer R; *Meaning Reconstruction and the Experience of Loss* (American Psychological Association; 2001)

Packman W, Horsley H, Davies B, Kramer R; *Continuing Bonds Following the Death of a Sibling* (Death Studies Journal; 2007) 30: 817-841.

Stambor Z; *Is Our Happiness Set in Stone?* (Monitor on Psychology; December 2007)

University of Michigan Depression Center (www.med.umich.edu/ depression/understanding_index2.htm)

University of Michigan Depression Self-Screening Online Diagnostic — (www.mentalhealthscreening.org/screening/welcome.asp)

The Stanford Forgiveness Project — (www.learningtoforgive.com/ about.htm)

• • •

"What we have once enjoyed we can
never lose. All that we love deeply
becomes a part of us."

— *Helen Keller*

About the Authors

eric Hipple was a National Football League (NFL) quarterback whose ten-year career was spent with the Detroit Lions. Eric's accomplishments include two playoff bids, a divisional championship, and the Detroit Lions' most valuable player award for the 1981 season. He is currently ranked fifth in career passing yards for Detroit. From

Eric Hipple with his co-authors,
Dr. Gloria Horsley (left) and
Dr. Heidi Horsley

1995-2000, Eric was color analyst for the Fox network NFL pregame show in Detroit.

Eric's life took a tragic turn when his 15-year-old son Jeff died of suicide in April 2000. Eric has since devoted his life to building awareness of and breaking down the stigma surrounding depressive illnesses. He has won numerous awards, including the Detroit Lions 2010 Courage House award, the prestigious 2008 Lifetime Achievement Award from the American Foundation for Suicide Prevention, and a presidential citation at the American Psychological Association's 2006 Annual Convention for his years of national community-based work combating adolescent depression and encouraging suicide prevention.

Eric is an outreach specialist for the University of Michigan Comprehensive Depression Center and serves on the national advisory board of the Open to Hope Foundation. His message of resilience has provided mental health awareness worldwide to professional groups, military, law enforcement, schools, and communities. Through the "Under the Helmet" program, Eric has reached out to thousands of high school and youth coaches across the country. Most recently, Eric was instrumental in forming a collaboration between the NFLPA Former Players and the University of Michigan Comprehensive Depression Center, in which the center serves as a destination site for evaluation and consultation.

Eric co-authored a study examining depression among retired football players; the study appeared in the April 2007 issue of *Medicine & Science in Sports & Exercise*. In addition, he was featured in a 2008 documentary and national community outreach program called *Men Get Depression* (www.mengetdepression.com). The film has been broadcast on public television stations across the U.S.

●　●　●

Gloria C. Horsley, Ph.D., M.F.C., C.N.S., is an internationally known grief expert, psychotherapist, and bereaved parent. She is a licensed Clinical Nurse Specialist and Marriage and Family Therapist. She co-hosts the popular syndicated Internet radio show, *Open to Hope,* heard weekly and archived on www.opentohope.com. Dr. Gloria serves as president of the Open to Hope Foundation, is on the national advisory board of The Compassionate Friends, and is a contributor to Maria Shriver's blog. She has been a faculty member of the University of Rochester School of Nursing and the Psychiatric Nursing Consultant to the Medical Center.

Dr. Gloria has made appearances on a number of television and radio shows, including *The Today Show.* She presents numerous seminars and workshops throughout the country. She has authored a multitude of articles and written several books. The books she has co-authored with her daughter Dr. Heidi Horsley include: *Open to Hope: Inspirational Stories of Healing After Loss; Open to Hope: Inspirational Stories for Handling the Holidays After Loss;* and *Teen Grief Relief: Parenting with Understanding, Support, and Guidance.*

* * *

Heidi Horsley, Psy.D., L.M.S.W., M.S., is a licensed psychologist, social worker, and bereaved sibling. She is an internationally known grief expert and is the executive director for the Open to Hope Foundation. Dr. Heidi co-hosts the syndicated talk radio show *Open to Hope* and has a private practice in New York City, specializing in grief and loss. She is an adjunct professor at Columbia University School of Social Work and serves on the national board of directors for The Compassionate Friends and on the advisory boards for the Tragedy Assistance Program for Survivors of Military Loss and Our Conservatory, a nonprofit music library for at-risk youths.

Dr. Heidi has appeared on ABC's *20/20,* and she has been interviewed by numerous radio stations, newspapers, and magazines, including the *Washington Post, Time Magazine,* and the *NY Daily News.* She worked for almost 10 years for the FDNY-Columbia University Family Guidance Program, a longitudinal study providing ongoing intervention to families of firefighters killed in the World Trade Center. In addition, she presents seminars throughout the country. Dr. Heidi has co-authored a number of books with her mother Dr. Gloria Horsley, including: *Open to Hope: Inspirational Stories of Healing After Loss; Open to Hope: Inspirational Stories for Handling the Holidays After Loss;* and *Teen Grief Relief: Parenting with Understanding, Support, and Guidance.*

Photo Gallery

Back in happier days, Eric celebrates his birthday amidst smiles from left to right: Jeff, Tarah, & Taylor.

Toddler Jeff with mom, Jann.

Erica & Jeff pose for Halloween.

Jeff & Eric enjoy a game of touch football in their back yard.

Christmas portrait of Jeff & Erica.

Jeff poses with sisters Erica (front),
Taylor (left), & Tarah.

The last photo taken of Jeff,
just days before his death.

Eric's girls help him celebrate his 50th birthday.
Left to right: wife Shelly; daughters Tarah, Taylor, & Erica.

Eric at his office at the University of
Michigan Depression Center.

131

How to Order

Quality of Life Publishing Co. specializes in inspirational and gentle grief support books for readers of all ages. Here's how to order *Real Men Do Cry* and other publications:

Bookstores: Available wherever books are sold

Online   www.QoLpublishing.com

Email: books@QoLpublishing.com

Phone: **1-877-513-0099**
Toll free in the U.S. and Canada
or call 1-239-513-9907during regular
business hours, Eastern Time.

Fax: **1-239-513-0088**

Mail: **Quality of Life Publishing Co.**
P.O. Box 112050
Naples, FL 34108-1929

Eric Hipple, author of *Real Men Do Cry,* speaks to groups of all sizes across the United States. Call us (toll free 1-877-513-0099) to bring Eric to your community.